D0478361

Praise for
Saint Everywhere

"What would it mean to live with the faith of a saint—either on a grand scale or in our own modest lives? With the effortless, heartfelt wit of Annie Lamott, Mary Lea Carroll whisks us along on a series of lively, serendipitous pilgrimages that leave us laughing, amazed, and ready to set off on our own miraculous adventures."

— PERDITA FINN, co-author of
The Way of the Rose

"*Saint Everywhere* is a gem of a book—delightful storytelling, factually fascinating, and spiritually uplifting. The right book for this moment in time when so many are on their own journey looking for the good in the everyday. I'm a fan of the lady saints, and now I'm a fan of Mary Lea Carroll. *Saint Everywhere* is a comfort and an inspiration."

— LIAN DOLAN, Satellite Sister
and author of *Elizabeth the First Wife*
and *Helen of Pasadena*

"Faith is a journey, and as Mary Lea Carroll shows in her delightful, insightful book, that journey can be both external and internal all at once"
— RICK HAMLIN, author of *Pray for Me* and executive editor of *Guideposts*

"Charming, funny, informative, moving and spiritually profound, this little book delights the soul."
— MICHELLE HUNEVEN, author of *Off Course*, *Blame*, and *Round Rock*

Saint Everywhere

TRAVELS IN SEARCH OF THE LADY SAINTS

MARY LEA CARROLL

Prospect Park Books

Published by Prospect Park Books
An imprint of Turner Publishing Company
www.prospectparkbooks.com
www.turnerbookstore.com

Distributed by Consortium Book Sales & Distribution
www.cbsd.com

Library of Congress Cataloging-in-Publication Data is on file with the Library of Congress. The following is for reference only:

Names: Carroll, Mary Lea, author.
Title: Saint Everywhere : travels in search of the lady saints / by Mary Lea Carroll.
Identifiers: LCCN 2018045632 (print) | LCCN 2018050371 (ebook) | ISBN 9781945551574 (Ebook) | ISBN 9781945551567 (hardback) | ISBN 9781684428380 (paperback)
Classification: LCC BR1713 (ebook) | LCC BR1713 .C37 2019 (print) | DDC 270.092/52--dc23
LC record available at https://lccn.loc.gov/2018045632
Subjects: Memoir / women saints / Christian shrines / travel

Illustrations by Joe Rohde
Cover design by David Ter-Avanesyan
Page design & layout by Amy Inouye, Future Studio
Printed in the United States of America

For Bill

"To reach something good, it is very useful to have gone astray, and thus acquired experience."

— St. Teresa of Avila

"Bizarre travel plans are dancing lessons
  from God."

— Kurt Vonnegut

Contents

Introduction

Pondering Life More

These stories go back and forth over eighteen years of my life, the years I spent raising children and helping my husband build his businesses. They reflect my growing desire to understand some of the reasons for being here, alive, on earth. When the book *Lean In* came out, urging women to step up their leadership in professional life, my initial response was, *Oh brother!* Women are already doing everything—now we also have to lean in? But all the talk about leaning in got me thinking about women who have had tremendous effects on this world, and yet, like so many, haven't gotten their due.

I decided to adopt a hobby: Wherever I was lucky enough to travel, if a shrine dedicated to a female saint was nearby, I would take myself there and make of it what I could. From my grandfather Cassidy's side of the family, my Catholic heritage goes back more than a thousand years. That is not an easy ship to jump from when the waters get rough, which they have been lately. In turning my eyes toward the women saints, I have found some fun, a lightness to the landscape where questions sprout everywhere—questions such as: So her body hasn't decomposed?

And she did what? With no money? And everybody said, no, no, no to her, but she did it anyway?

I didn't pre-select these lady saints. In a way, they selected me—I made the trek to see their shrines or miraculous sites only if my travels had brought me nearby. These "treks to go see" became enchanting alternatives to the repetitive realities of regular life. I could let my mind trip around between the seen and unseen worlds. These little adventures built up a fire in me for something I'd always had, but now have in infinitely richer ways: a love of God. These travels have taken me deep into God's world, coloring every aspect of my day. It's gorgeous and it's weird. And I have my time with the lady saints to thank for that.

A saint is a person who, when alive, did extraordinarily amazing things for...well, us all, really. Bestowing sainthood on someone is the Church's way of acknowledging this. And as I've gotten to know some of these women of history whose works live on, I've found the Church's acknowledgments to be more than deserved.

So...let's take an adventure together and wonder over the strange and inspiring achievements of gals who not only leaned in and broke glass ceilings, they actually bent reality.

One

Come Fly with Me!

St. Catherine of Siena
1347–1380
Siena, Italy

How the trail of the lady saints opened up:

"What if you and Bill came with me to Italy?" my father-in-law asked cheerfully over the phone one Saturday morning. "I'm going with my veterans' group." John was eighty. The year was 2000, a new millennium was starting, and World War II veterans were passing away at a rate of a thousand a year. Bill never took vacations, being the owner of a Hollywood company that makes trailers, the coming attractions for movies. But even he knew that this took precedence over work. We decided to bring our oldest daughter, twelve-year-old Glenn Mary, along with us, leaving her two younger sisters home in good care. We would be visiting battle sites, village to village, in the hills around Florence. We'd learn how the 10th Mountain Division finally drove the Germans out from what is, today, a lot of pretty Italian ski towns. Pretty ski towns with new buildings and hotels, because there was little left but wreckage after the war. The medieval stone-on-stone look of these hill towns was forever erased.

Before long there we were, packed into a bus full of veterans and their families, motoring among the lovely hills. Our group archivist gave us historical background: "Okay, around the next bend, on February 19th of '45, the 10th advanced up Mt. Belvedere—right over there—before dawn."

John leaned over and whispered to me, "There wasn't a tree on this mountain then. Completely shelled. No cover at all. All these trees have grown since the war."

The archivist continued, "For six months we had been stymied in this valley, unable to dislodge the German fortifications from Riva Ridge, up over there. But that day, the 10th Mountain took Riva Ridge, and then swiftly the next day, Mt. Belvedere, in one of the most daring escapades of the war. It cost 1,000 lives. Tomorrow, we will all hike up to the top of Mt. Belvedere, those who are able. We'll have a nice ceremony and a picnic." I looked around the bus at the number of hardy octogenarians and was glad I'd been exercising. I *might* be able to keep up with them on our hike up the mountain.

The people of Lizzano in Belvedere, an adjacent city, still remember their rescue from the Germans. They'd hospitably prepared lunch for us in the town square. Shopkeepers, kids on bikes, old men on benches, lots of young people from the curb— everyone stared at us with open curiosity as we ate pasta and salads at long tables. We listened to the mayor's speech of thanks. Time evaporated as I felt the gross horror of those wartime days, when Italy was more like Iraq than a tourist's delight, when our boys died in the rocky, dusty dirt so far from home. These elderly men in golf shirts, our fathers, were what remained of the force that liberated this very town. My father-in-law quietly recounted, between bites of lunch, how he'd been resting on a stone step at the edge of this very square when a sniper's bullet killed the soldier sitting next to him. Then he chuckled and said, "I like Italy a lot better now," pointing to a giant red basket of geraniums hanging so prettily from the lamppost. I knew from family stories that John was among the first soldiers to make it to the top alive and take out the foxholes up the mountain we would later climb.

For five days we retraced the steps of the 10th Mountain Division's advance up through the Florentine hill towns and into the Po Valley. Every town you've never heard of had black granite war memorials chiseled with American names—John Willis, Michael Spence, Bill Andrews, and on and on. I couldn't stop looking at all the ice cream shops, racks of post-cards, and cute boutiques in these towns, feeling chilled by the difference between peace and war, love and hatred.

When it was time for us to part company from the veterans' tour, we hugged and kissed John good-bye, hopped into a rental car, and headed to Siena—a place I knew nothing about, but everyone had said, "It's beautiful, it's old, go there!" I had a vague idea there was a St. Catherine of Siena, because so many churches are named...St. Catherine of Siena.

Well, you just cannot do better than sipping a steaming cappuccino at a café on the sprawling Piazza del Campo while your daughter writes postcards and your husband studies maps. It seemed like the most beautiful public space in the world. I watched the shade working its way across the medieval buildings that ring the square, imagining the jousting and the market days and the politi-cal rallies Piazza del Campo has seen over its 900 years, not to mention the medieval horse race that careens around the plaza to this day. I looked at the amiable American and German tourists strolling by and imagined them in World War II uniforms—how they'd been shooting and stabbing each other fifty-five years earlier. I sipped a little more cappucci-no and the uniforms dissolved into the velvet tunics or sackcloth of the Middle Ages. My mind danced across the centuries. Oh, this cappuccino was good in its heavy white porcelain cup. I snuggled deeper into the wicker café chair, lost in the lines of arched windows looking down on the piazza, the crooked terra-cotta roofs, the pleasure of the moment.

Our hotel room, up, up, up stairs and in the back of a fourteenth-century palace, offered a spectacular view from the tiniest window over the bathtub. From there we could see endless yellow fields and far-off stone towers. With a hum of pleasure, I realized there was no way to tell what century it was.

"Let's go see the saint's remains!" I proposed to Bill and Glennie. Bill was stretched out on the fluffy bed, resting after driving us here.

He gave a little groan, mumbling, "Saint's remains? Honey, we're on vacation."

Undaunted, I opened the Fodor's guidebook. I summarized, "Parts of St. Catherine are on display in the twelfth-century Basilica of San Domenico's, a main tourist attraction...."

"Parts," Bill seemed to say to himself. It started raining as we headed out and hurried across the slippery cobblestones, one of those summer storms with violent thunder and a crazy five-minute downpour.

San Domenico is a medieval construction of brick and stone, fearfully plain and austere. We scuttled in out of the wet. So dark and expansive was the inside that we all suddenly felt lost. Its interior vastness made people seem like ants milling about. I placed a hand on a pillar to steady myself and proceeded to tilt my head back as far as I could. I could barely see the gloomy upper recesses. Suddenly, through the thirty-foot windows, came a blast of lightning, followed instantly by exploding thunder. The huge space boomed. Everyone was knocked off balance with an "Ohhh!" My jaw clenched. God Himself might be saying, "*Oh, it's you! Nice.*"

A group of people knelt before a small side altar that flickered with votive candles. Nudging my way in and around, like I do for the Rose Parade on New Year's Day back home in Pasadena, I saw an ancient crystal case holding a frayed velvet cushion. A silver filigree holder sat on the red cushion and in the holder was—*St. Catherine's thumb*. It looked like a stub of charcoal sporting a fingernail. It was 620 years old! They said her head was here too, somewhere, but it turned out it was on long-term loan to Rome—in fact, for 300 years already.

I love, love, love this kind of thing. It is all just so strange and kind of fun and yet so very mysterious. I wanted to know why, for hundreds and hundreds of years, people have revered Catherine? Why are parish churches all over the world named after her? I knelt down and thought, Who *are* you? And—*Hello*—why hasn't your thumb turned to dust?

Well, I bought the little booklet to find out. For the next three nights, I stayed up late, reading. There's something so great about sitting up in a cozy hotel bed, not sleepy at all, reading while everyone around you sleeps. It's so freeing, like you have all the time in the world.

Catherine was born in 1347, the youngest of twenty-five children. Her father was a well-to-do wool dyer. She grew up on Via dei Tintori, which wasn't far from our hotel. Detailed accounts of her life came from interviews with her mother, neighbors, and friends, as well as a biography written by her life-long friend and confessor, Raimondo of Capua. He'd been present at her death and was actually the one who dismembered her body (now, that's a friend) so that parts of her could be sent to different cathedrals, as was the way with saints in medieval times.

It all began for Catherine when she was six years old, walking with her brothers toward San Domenico's, the very church that holds her thumb. She looked up, and in the sky above the basilica, she saw a vision of Jesus sitting on a throne, saints Peter and Paul on either side. The vision was bathed in shining light, and the intense pleasure she received gave her the desire to pray incessantly so she could see even more. From that age, she prayed day and night, seeking solitude, seeking a road to that great feeling of pleasure and peace she'd caught a glimpse of. By the time she was fifteen, she wanted only to be in seclusion in her tiny bedroom—praying, meditating, and learning directly from Jesus, all the while in a growing mystical union with Him. As she grew older, she still refused to leave her prayer room, and no matter how much her parents tried to find her a husband, she refused to marry.

Then, at the age of eighteen, she left her seclusion and rejoined her family to cook and clean as if she were their servant. Her parents tried to stop her from doing this, but she said she *must* be their servant. Her mother worried about her ever-stranger daughter. Catherine wouldn't sleep, barely ate, and went into ecstatic trances. I thought of how my own mother fretted when my teenage brother, back in the sixties, refused to wear shoes, use a fork, cut his hair, and go to school. He was most definitely not on the road to sainthood, but mothers everywhere, in every age, worry about their strange children.

Catherine began serving the poor and the ill, mostly by taking anything she wanted from her father's house to give to the less fortunate. Curiously, the more she gave away, the more the family seemed to have. No matter how much wine she gave away, their barrel was never empty. No matter how much bread she baked and gave away, the flour sack was always full. She took this as a sign that she needed to do even more. I read this at an afternoon stop in a *gelateria*, a little shop with many varieties of lovely ice cream. I underlined that part in my booklet. I love this version of the generous life: No matter how much you give, there is always plenty. I gazed into the refrigerated display case full of every flavor of ice cream and could almost see St. Catherine laughing and scooping it out left and right to us hot, cranky tourists, the stainless-steel tubs never getting low. Going out into public was exhausting to Catherine after her years of solitude. But that early glimpse of heaven and her desire to love God through loving others propelled her. "The road to heaven *is* heaven," she's quoted as saying.

In those days, Siena had a hospital that was already 200 years old. Much of the medical practice at La Scala Hospital reached back into the Dark Ages: wine and oil poured over open wounds, poultices of flowers and leaves, bitter herb potions. Medical practice mostly dealt with comforting the dying and being amazed if someone actually got well. Catherine worked long and hard cleaning, comforting, and praying over people who had horrible burns, infected broken bones, full-body open sores, and leprosy. She was fearless because she felt that the sooner she herself died, the sooner she could go to heaven. Her desire to get this life over with so she could get on to the next is not so appealing to our modern sensibilities. Let me skip past this part.

Before long, citizens began to notice this young woman who spent all morning at Mass, then spent the rest of the day moving swiftly, almost like she could fly, through all parts of the city, helping here, helping there. In fact, there are many accounts of her *actually* flying. Up a staircase. Across a public square. Or, wildly, physically being in two places at once. There is an account in which Catherine was on retreat in a monastery and yet was also in a prison cell, praying for a notorious murderer to repent before he was hanged. Talk about multitasking! And then there are the many accounts of how she levitated while in ecstatic meditation. Her ecstasies were so common that friends would grow impatient waiting for her to come back. I can just hear them, *"Catherine, come on, we're late—we've been waiting, like, forever! Let's get going!"* Her friends, who didn't receive visions, would harrumph around wondering why God wasn't gifting them with trances, too. I've actually always wondered why some people have such simple, clear faith in God and others have such uncertainty and conflict about faith. They say faith is a gift, but is it really? Just a gift?

Catherine's life evolved from the privacy of her home to tending the needy in the streets, and then to admirers gathering around her for advice and direction on the problems of life. Through her constant prayer and dialogues with Jesus in ecstatic mysticism, God granted her the ability to see straight into the souls of others. People were amazed by her ability to understand their true thoughts and feelings. She could speak to the secret movements of their minds. When Catherine was in the presence of truly good people, she'd be smitten by the beauty of their souls. Conversely, when she met people who were corrupt, guilty, and anger-filled, she'd cringe and end up vomiting from their smell. And those were just during her formative years—her early to mid-twenties—the years when most people are fooling around, drinking too much, and trying to figure things out. When she approached her late twenties, things really started to happen.

Catherine never officially learned to read or write, yet she either dictated or wrote while in a trance more than 400 letters displaying an eloquence and details of daily life that are the finest record of Tuscan life in the thirteenth century.

Then came bad times for the city of Siena. Political parties rioted against one another, and big family groups across the city went after one another, as in Shakespeare's *Romeo and Juliet*. The emperor and the pope got into a fight over to whom the city owed its allegiance. Anarchy and armed battle broke out all over. It was said the city was a bubbling witch's cauldron of hatred and violence. Now Catherine's chief work became making peace. Her verbal powers, her fearlessness, her aura of love, and her persuasiveness proved effective against the arrogance, worldliness, and hatred of the warring men.

She began sending her letters to the battling princes of Siena and Florence demanding that they stop, that they repent. Her moral authority was so potent that it worked. She quelled the violence. A woman on her own, changing history. Letters next went to bishops who had fallen into all sorts of dastardly behaviors: taking mistresses, eating and drinking themselves practically to death, gambling, spending, partying. She attacked the problem with such forceful reason, eloquence, and love that she shamed them into reform. She then wrote the pope himself, Gregory XI, asking him to restore morality and respect to the church: to come back from Avignon, where the papacy was then based, to rescue Rome. These letters seemed to fall on deaf ears, so she traveled to Avignon. She reasoned with and implored Pope Gregory to return the papacy to Rome after almost 100 years of debauchery under the sway of French kings. She, an unmarried laywoman, not even a nun, with no formal education, eventually convinced him.

On September 13, 1376, the pope sailed back to Rome. Catherine, she walked back. Today it's a nine-hour car ride from Avignon to Rome. I know people were hardier in the past, but she constantly fasted and denied herself even water for days. How did a woman in the thirteenth century have the strength to walk all that way? Honestly, even with my expensive walking shoes, one day on the cobblestone streets did my feet in. I thought about the myriad little helpers I have to make life easier: a little pillbox of Tylenol and sleep aids, eye drops for itchy eyes, a window air conditioner in our hotel room, my purse with its wide comfort strap. I had no interest in denying myself any of them.

Catherine was known for extreme forms of self-discipline, which she considered a way to put herself in close union with her soul. It was part of her desire to be with Christ, so close as to *be* Christ when performing her works of love and charity. She considered her physical body a hindrance. Many nights she slept only half an hour. She lived on vegetables and bitter herbs. She willingly embraced disgusting and/or frightful acts of charity, like washing the boils of the sick or entering the rooms of the dying to comfort them when others were too afraid due to the blood or smell or shrieks of pain. She had no fear of such dirty jobs as wiping up vomit and preparing bodies for burial. Strangely, as eyewitnesses recounted, her hands always remained clean and only became more beautiful the harder she worked.

Each day we were in Siena, I became more and more intrigued by Catherine. I stayed up later and later reading.

Her *Dialogue* book stands out even today. It contains conversations between her soul and God about the spiritual life. In the field of psychology, these early writings are regarded as groundbreaking, the first time thought processes were so deeply explored. She wrote, "Soul, as a quality of style, is a fact." St. Catherine's soul expressed itself so winningly, so sweetly, so reasonably that she was an irresistible friend. She intuitively perceived life in the highest possible forms: beauty and love. She was a permanent source of strength to all who knew her. That, I realized, is what those who'd been praying at her altar in San Domenico's were doing: seeking strength and inspiration from her.

Catherine is the patron saint of Italy, along with St. Francis of Assisi. In 1970, Pope Paul VI proclaimed her a Doctor of the Church because of her contribution to theology and spiritual writings and her ability to speak truth to power. In 1999, Pope John Paul II made her the co-patron saint of Europe, along with a few other amazing people from the past who I'd never heard of, including St. Bridget of Sweden, the thirteenth-century noblewoman who made it her business to single-handedly raise the moral tone of her era, and the incredible Edith Stein, who was born Jewish, became a Carmelite nun, and ended up dying in the Nazi death chambers. Other co-patron saints of Europe are Benedict, known for his fifth-century monastic *Rule*, writings that advocate a balanced life of prayer, work, and rest, and the siblings Cyril and Methodius, who in the fourth century invented an alphabet and brought Christianity and learning to the Slavs.

Our beautiful hotel room had a double bed for us and a little side bed for Glennie. Heavy starched white sheets. You could hear footsteps on the cobblestones below and voices of those walking by. I love the giant feather pillows European hotels have.

"Mary Lea, put that crazy St. Catherine book

down. It's late," Bill mumbled sleepily.

"Honey! It's awesome. Listen to this: 'At one point, St. Catherine experienced Jesus coming to her so intensely that he literally reached into her heart, plucked it out—*her heart!*—and replaced it with his own, which was on fire!' "

From Bill, under the covers, "That's just crazy."

And me, in reply—"I know!"

From Glennie, under the covers, "Mom, turn off the light."

So I did. But I pondered in the dark this whole implausible tale of St. Catherine. Do I believe it? It's hard to say yes. But I *want* to believe. Life seems bigger, grander, more fun if you believe that a person can have mystical powers. That one woman can quell a war. That something horrible like Germans and Americans wanting to kill each other, as we did in World War II, can change, did change, to two peoples wishing each other well.

Catherine of Siena died when she was thirty-three years old, in the year 1380. An ambassador, a peacemaker, a woman of letters, and, apparently, a woman who could fly. I drifted off to sleep thinking about, of all people, Oscar Wilde. That famous epigram attributed to him: "Be yourself, everyone else is already taken." St. Catherine said it 500 years earlier: "Be who God meant you to be and you will set the world on fire."

Too soon we were back home in Pasadena. Ten-year-old Grace and six-year-old Rosie were waiting for us. Our dear friend Brigid had been watching them, and only one mishap occurred: The pet rats, Venus and Mars, had escaped and were now livin' *la vida loca* under the deck outside. (This ultimately became a pretty crazy problem.)

The little girls opened their gifts of red ladybug necklaces, purchased from the jewelry stalls on the Ponte Vecchio in Florence. I loved being home, in our beautiful 100-year-old Craftsman. I know every bush by name in my rose garden and every neighbor by name on our tree-lined street. But, wistfully, I realized that the beautiful mental expansiveness I'd had while traveling would be eaten up in a nanosecond, what with reading aloud in the girls' school, making the soccer snacks, doing what I could for Bill's business, helping one brother who needed a kidney transplant and another who was divorcing, and keeping up with our friends, not to mention the infestation hell that Venus and Mars had created. These things take over. But for a long time my mind churned on the juicy facts of St. Catherine, which ultimately led me to other lady saints.

"You are rewarded not according to your work or your time but according to the measure of your love."

— ST. CATHERINE OF SIENA

Two

Olor de las Rosas

(The Scent of Roses)
The Visionaries of Medju...Medju-*what*?
Glendale, California

About a year after my visit with St. Catherine, my friend Teresa called. She and I were Girl Scout mom-friends—her daughter and Glennie belonged to the same eighth-grade troop. They went to St. Elizabeth's, the same elementary school I had attended and for some karmic reason felt compelled to send my children to. (You can do that sort of thing if you live less than a mile from where you were born, as I do. Because I have always been a world traveler, living right where I was born is a lucky comfort.)

"Mary Lea, want to come to Incarnation Church in Glendale on Thursday night?" Teresa asked. "One of the visionaries from Medjugorje is coming. He's going to give a little talk, we'll all say the rosary, and he'll have a vision."

Being raised Catholic has its drawbacks. It's like living in the same house your whole life, no adventure of discovery. That's why the wilder side of Catholicism appeals to me. Saints' heads in Rome, visionaries, Mary appearing in towns and tortillas... it gives me plenty to chew on.

"Teresa, I'd love to, but Medju-*what?*"

"You know, the town in Bosnia where the Virgin's been appearing every day since 1981." She explained that back then, eight children claimed that the Virgin had appeared to them, asking them to bring messages to the world—and most of these eight people, now in their fifties, say she still visits them daily! The messages they deliver, through trances, are followed by millions around the world. One of these eight was coming to, of all places, Glendale, California.

Intriguing. A real live visionary. One of LA's many midsize satellite cities, Glendale is just ten minutes west of Pasadena, over the hills of Eagle Rock. It has none of the big attractions Pasadena has—Caltech, the Rose Bowl, the Norton Simon— but it's where I bought my beloved Subaru, and it's got the locally famous café/bakery Porto's, and now it was getting a visit from a visionary.

A coffee stop at Porto's puts you into the caffeinated crossroads of the world. Mexicans, Armenians, Chinese, Polish, Africans, Peruvians, Filipinos, *and*

Pasadenans—we all jostle at the Cuban café, indulging in the sweet life. Down a leafy street not far from Porto's, I found the neighborly Incarnation Church.

How packed this average-size church was on a Thursday night! It seemed that lots of people knew about this Bosnian place I couldn't pronounce. We were squeezed in shoulder to shoulder, and though I saw Teresa and her husband, Jorge, there was no way to get to them. All the aisles were jammed. People were still flooding in.

I wedged myself into a pew—not too close to the altar, not too far away, the safe middle. I wished I knew more about the visionaries and even where this place was. But with no fanfare, we were all suddenly off and away into the rosary.

As I have gotten older, the rosary has gotten shorter, it seems, and when said in perfect unison by 400 people, all our voices pulling together like oarsmen on a ship, rowing up and down the Hail Marys in the harmonic way this ancient prayer does when repeated over and over, every worry can evaporate. Having a repetitive prayer or even just a phrase is an excellent way to calm the mind. All spiritual practices have some form of this; mental-health experts advise us all to practice meditation, which is not religious at all. The rosary, a string of beads used to count the repeated Hail Marys, helps people get into a deep meditation on the mysteries of faith and life. The rosary is still widely used today, 900 years after St. Dominic brought it to popularity.

After each decade, or set of ten Hail Marys, one of the real live visionaries, Ivan Dragicevic, asked us to pause. He told us how the Virgin loves us. How her message of peace is intended for us. How we must trust in her love. And then we'd start up again with more Hail Marys. This had gone on for about fifteen minutes when I was jolted from my reverie by a huge, dime-store-quality shot of rose perfume.

My eyes popped open. I sniffed around. Yes, definitely, it was roses. But why wasn't anyone else stirring? Well, so, whatever…I closed my eyes again and commenced again, but then, there it was again, as if it had been sprayed right on me. My eyes popped open again, and I turned all the way around in my place, wondering, *What the heck?* Then I understood—they put atomizers in the air conditioning ducts to give everyone a goose of special effects right at the most meditative stage of the rosary. But why wasn't anyone else reacting?

Then it happened a third time, and I kept my eyes closed. *Wait,* I thought—*is this just for me? Ohhh.*

The Bosnian visionary was the most ordinary-looking of men: balding, nice slacks, sports coat, pudgy. He concluded the rosary. The music started as he sat down. He stared up into the air above him. He was motionless, and the music died. You could hear a pin drop. A feeling had been filling this church since we began the rosary, and now it was thick in the air. You could feel it: love, an actual substance. For some reason I thought of a new jar of peanut butter and how you can dig a knife into it and smear heavy goodness across a piece of bread. Something had spread love across all of us. We were in it together, me and 399 other strangers—well, except for Teresa and Jorge, who were 300 people away from me.

When he finally spoke, the Bosnian man simply said, "Our Lady loves you all. She needs you to pray more. She needs each of you to create more love in this world. It can only be done by you. Work on your soul the way you work on other aspects of yourself. You go to the gym for your body. You go to school for your mind. Do not neglect your soul. You must pray more. She wishes each of you to spread more peace. She wishes for each of you to spread more love." I sat there, still waiting for the real message—you know, some kind of bombshell from beyond—but that was it. He stood up and smiled and thanked us all for attending, and now it was time to wiggle my way out of this sardine can, inch by inch up the center aisle.

I fell in next to a tiny Latino lady, and I asked, "Señora, did you...smell...anything during the rosary?"

Her eyes lit up and she beamed a smile. "Oh yes. Roses."

"You smelled them!"

"Oh yes. The Virgin is here."

"But no one else seemed to notice!"

"I know. But I did. It's a special thing," she said.

"It is?" I asked. Had I experienced a phenomenon? Had I received a gift? Roses. The name rosary comes from "rosarium," a collection of rose garlands. And of course, I've always loved roses; who doesn't? Practically every early morning I'm out in my own rose garden having a glory moment with *Julia Child* and *Hot Coco* and *Barbara Streisand,* to name a few of my forty-plus bushes.

Roses are the most gifted flower on earth. They were found woven into funeral wreaths in the Egyptian tombs. They are the instant symbol of love or sorrow or celebration. Rose essential oil is powerful against depression and helpful with— good news—libido. I went home and told my family about smelling the roses and about the visionary from Medju-wherever.

Bill couldn't help it. I could see Doubting Thomas just leap into his eyes. Extreme patience came over him.

"Oh, I know all about Medjugorje," said Rosie, my fourth grader.

"You do?!"

"Poor Andrew Ivankovich. He's had to do a report on it like every year since kindergarten."

"You're kidding, Rosie—why?"

"Because he's related to one of the visionaries. It's his dad's cousin or second uncle or something."

How could so many people know about this

place that I'm just hearing about right now?

Years passed, and Medjugorje kept coming in and out of my mind. Finally, a couple of years ago, I went through my office and dug out an old elementary school roster and looked up Andrew's parents, Nancy and Ivan Ivankovich. It had been ages since we'd socialized, but I called up Nancy and invited them for dinner. After a lot of missed calls and texts, it was all arranged, and now we were sitting down over a bottle of wine. After a respectable amount of chitchat I launched in, "Ivan. Are you really related to one of the visionaries?" He paused. Ivan was in his early fifties and a successful tech startup financier. Finally, he chuckled, nodded, and tried to explain.

"My dad left Medjugorje in 1963. Everyone is sort of cousins there. It was so small, maybe 300 people, and I'm exactly the same age as the kids who saw the Virgin. They were like eight to sixteen years old. We went back in 1974 to visit and I played ball in the street with all those kids. They were just regular kids." Ivan spread his hands on the table before him. "We went back again in 1983 and they were different. They carried rosaries around in their pockets and prayed all the time. I don't know what happened, but something changed them." Ivan just shrugged and shook his head. "Ivanka Ivankovich—one of the visionaries—is my grandfather's first wife's granddaughter. I'm actually closer to Ivan Dragicevic, though. We aren't related, but

I know him better. We have coffee when we're in the same city." I marveled that I had two degrees of separation right here at my own dining room table.

I had to ask. "What do you make of it? Do you believe it?" Here, he lost his words. He shook his head—not no, but thinking, wrestling with his rational mind.

"Something happened there. I cannot say what." He threw up his hands. "But it's a very good thing."

I was hoping to make sense of it, these inexplicable occurrences in a tiny tobacco-farming village. Could it be that the Virgin Mary really began appearing to a few kids fooling around on a hill one summer day? Most of them still say they receive daily visitations that last two to eight minutes. Mary kindly and gently asks them again and again to pray for peace, to pray for increased faith, to pray for our families. That's all good, *but I have so many questions*!

And also, where again is this place?

Three

If You Build It, They Will Come

ST. FRANCES XAVIER CABRINI
1850–1917
New York City and
the Rocky Mountains, Colorado

"I'm going off to meet someone," I said to Bill as I kissed him goodbye. He nodded his head as he turned the page of the sports section. "Be back in a few hours." He reached for the TV clicker as I said, "Don't forget to check on the theater tickets." He nodded again, settling in for Soccer Sunday.

I've jetted ahead, over many milestones, to 2013. Bill and I had rented an apartment for an entire month to see what living in the Big Apple was like. After all, the kids were doing fine, what with Rosie in college and Glennie and Grace establishing their early careers. Bill had just sold his business. Retirement and empty nesthood were giving us so much freedom! Bill was usually happy on the couch, but

I've always wanted to be out and about. The thing is, he was exhausted by the years of owning and running a business. He'd often said that having payroll to meet was like having a hungry shark at his back all the time.

I headed for the elevator, but once I was on the street and halfway down the block, I realized I didn't know where I was going. Better ask.

"Now write this down," said the big African American man attending an apartment building's front door. We stood on 72nd Street on the Upper West Side, and I'd stopped to ask his advice. He put his gloved hand on my arm and pointed over to Broadway. "Ya gotta take the 1 train up past Harlem to 168th, then switch to the A train and go all the way up to 190th. Take the elevator up three floors and it'll let you out at Fort Tryon. You'll get it from there." Excited, I headed on, warmed by his taking the time with me. I nodded a greeting to a woman named Alice. She sat on a little pile of blankets by the subway entrance, and I saw her every day. So much is awful about every part of homelessness, including how it hardens the hearts of us passersby, who become numb and sometimes oblivious to the monumental suffering.

New York subway stops are such a trip—some so spotlessly clean, with espresso carts, and others all banged up and neglected, like this stop at 190th, packed with people rushing through narrow, dank, mine-like tunnels, up and then down tiny, steep steps. Big batches of us humans had to wait, existentially, until a freight elevator took us somewhere that hopefully was up, but I was too disoriented to know. I just rushed along with everyone else, feeling like water being pushed through a pipe, trusting that the crowd knew how to get out. And then we were out, let free into the wide-open sunlight and almost rural world of northern Manhattan. Few people were about. Big trees made for a nice neighborhood, and up the block was the sixties-era, red-brick Mother Cabrini High School.

I needed to see this with my own eyes. I'd heard this girls' school actually had St. Mother Cabrini's preserved body, all laid out in the school chapel. Now *that's* a school mascot! The motto on the school read:

Empowering Young Women of Culturally Diverse Backgrounds to Become Leaders and to Grow in Mind, Character, Heart, and Soul Since 1899

I was trying to think of everything I knew about St. Mother Cabrini. My mind took a turn back to my own daughters' high school years. Middle daughter Grace had entered the Mother Cabrini essay contest with the topic: "If you could change the world for the better, what would you do?" She wrote eloquently about the humane treatment of pets, and I wasn't going to suggest that she perhaps beef up her theme. If ever there was a girl who loved pets, it was her. Well, the girl who ended up winning received $250 and was invited to a luncheon at the LA Country Club. That pretty much covered all I knew of Mother Cabrini.

I tiptoed into the school, past a couple of full classrooms and the principal's office and toward the doors labeled with the sign "Shrine." I didn't want to hassle with all the visitor/name badge stuff if I could just slip in, quiet-like. Information pamphlets were on hand at a nearby table.

Spacious and midcentury modern with all its blond wood, the shrine was 100% empty. I sat and read the pamphlet. Mother Frances Xavier Cabrini, the first naturalized American citizen to become a saint, was a tiny woman from Italy. Born in 1850, she started out as a teacher in her small town, teaching and praying and making herself available to God's will. By the time she was thirty, she had formed herself into an authentic mystic. She believed she was destined to be a missionary. While still in her homeland, she founded an order of nuns, an orphanage, and two schools. At age forty, with three other nuns, she followed her true wish and emigrated to America to become a missionary to its Italian immigrants.

Lower Manhattan in the 1890s was the most densely populated place on earth, with squalid tenements and reeking, open sewers. Italians were pouring in at the rate of 100,000 a year. Many were sick, and most arrived with nothing. They were very much not wanted by their new nation. WOPS, they were called—With-Out-Papers. It would take generations for them to work their way into the everyday fabric of America. This was the scene for Mother Cabrini and her nuns when they straggled out of steerage and into the teeming streets of New York. No English, almost no money, and simply a letter of introduction to Bishop Corrigan. And then, because of a dispute and a misunderstanding between Bishop Corrigan and her bishop back home, she was told she couldn't stay, and that there was nothing there for her.

She and her companions would not take no for an answer. The four nuns found lodging among the Italians in the tenements, and she set about her business: setting up a classroom, establishing a prayer ministry, taking care of the sick. Accounts of her personality say she could make friends with anybody, she slept only three hours a night, and she was extremely stubborn. Over time, in this new land, her skill with money became something of an amazement. According to her diary, her entire focus was to improve the lives of the poor and displaced through God's love. She considered herself merely an obedient instrument of this love and took no credit for her achievements. She would simply say, "With Him, all things are possible."

Well, it was like she was let loose into this big, new land. In just twenty-seven years, she figured out a way to create sixty-seven institutions all across America, from New York to Los Angeles: academic and industrial schools, orphanages, hospitals, clinics, and prayer centers. And here she was, laid out in a glass casket, in this girls' high school chapel.

Mother Cabrini died in 1917 but was remarkably preserved in her black nun's habit on a satin cushion under the altar. I moved in closer, captivated. This wasn't actually her whole body, I'd learned from the info pamphlet. Her head and her heart were in Rome. (Note to self: Find out about heads and hearts being sent to Rome.) But what a great waxen head she had on her! I marveled, getting right up next to the casket. I knelt down and wanted to pray, but my mind could only dart about the spectacle before me: the folds of her woolen clothes, which I scanned for moth holes (I couldn't find any), her tiny, pointy *Wizard of Oz* leather shoes, how her wax face needed makeup, how hot and itchy her long habit looked. How dead she looked. How we all will die. How she'd been lying on this satin cushion since 1917. How the heck could one woman found all those institutions? Plus missions in Central and South America? *How?*

Suddenly, loud and crazy, the senior class of Mother Cabrini High School poured into the chapel. "Ladies, ladies, take a seat. Quiet down," came the voice of a heavy-set Latino man in a pink striped shirt. The senior class advisor? "Shhh," he said. "We are in the shrine." And really, these eighty inner-city girls, in their navy-blue uniforms, quieted right down. "Okay, we've fixed the issue with your transcripts. You can start sending them out to colleges. And about the Halloween party—I want you to have a special senior year, and I need you to meet me halfway. Look at those costumes at Party City. Two-thirds of them are not worth the money. They are not appropriate. Yes, you can bring a male guest, but I didn't invite the male schools because I don't want big groups of guys to deal with. Work with me, ladies. Let's make it special. Cost is $5. Those who can't do it, come talk to me."

I glanced at the shining black and brown faces of the girls. They all had a chance, and it made me love the efforts of the Catholic high schools. My own three daughters had benefited from a Catholic high school. I know firsthand the transformation girls go through during the high school years. I was happy for these girls, because they were in good hands. Suddenly, they all got up and left. Lunch time. It was just me and Mother Cabrini again, the saint who'd started this very school and was still influencing these very girls....

In display cases in the back, I saw a leather belt embedded with nails that she must have used for self-mortification or penance (glad those days are over), a silver hairbrush, and some of her dental gold. Lots of letters thanking Mother Cabrini for restoring wellness and granting favors. Her starched aprons and shirts. It's all kind of strange. The black-and-white photographs of Mother Cabrini make her look like an eerie ghost. That's a sharp contrast to the accounts of her personality, telling of a woman with superhuman energy, charm, and vision.

After poking around a side chapel, where you can light battery-operated candles, I decided it was time to walk across to Fort Tryon, a rugged, vast parkland that hugs the cliffs of northern Manhattan. It is home to the Cloisters: an honest-to-goodness thirteenth-century monastery, brought here stone by stone in the 1930s and now a museum filled with carved altars and the famous unicorn tapestries. I didn't want to go in that day. I wanted to stand on the high edge of Manhattan, awestruck by the flow of the Hudson River, the brush of autumn across the hills. I wanted to think more about how one woman could do so much for so many, even now, so many years after her death.

My mind ran over just the orphanages, hospitals, and schools I'd read or heard about: Columbus hospitals in New York, Chicago, and Seattle, three elementary schools in New York, Queen of Heaven Orphanage in Denver, Cabrini High School in New Orleans, various sanatoriums, and Regina Coeli Orphanage in Los Angeles. Taking her legacy up to today, her surviving works include Cabrini Immigration Services, Cabrini Action and Advocacy Coalition, Cabrini College, Cabrini Eldercare, spiritual ministries in Chicago, New York, and Colorado, and various retreat centers. My head became over-full, and I wanted coffee. Ugh, I was out in the middle of nature. I turned, wistfully fantasizing a coffee cart to materialize.

But hey! A stone house was just across the open space. I happily realized it had been converted into a restaurant with a view. Perfect! Taking a seat at the almost-empty bar, I ordered a cup of black coffee, which arrived perfectly in a white cup and saucer. *It should be perfect*, I thought ruefully, *it cost more than $5*—more than what some of those girls could afford for their dance. But there's just something great about a simple, bold cup of coffee. I sipped and thought. What is different about someone like me or you and someone who grows up to do such enormous deeds? Is there anyone like Mother Cabrini today who can make so much happen? There are many powerful women today. But how many are so purely obsessed with alleviating suffering? How many ask, *What does God want of me?* I sipped away, lost in the view. I waited for cosmic instructions, so afraid that God would say, *"Mary Lea, go down to the freeway and gather up all those mentally ill, addicted homeless people and create a solution.... Mary Lea, invent elderly housing that includes pets and children and purpose, not just block buildings decorated like cruise ships.... Mary Lea, what about all the autistic kids* *coming into adulthood.... Mary Lea, the guns—"*

Luckily a commotion at the end of the bar halted my overactive thinking. The only other customers in the place, a couple sitting a few stools away, had ordered champagne. She was hugging him; they looked elated. Startled, I realized he had just proposed, had just that very instant slipped a ring onto her finger. I eyed the waiter to see if I was right, and he nodded a sly smile. Wow! I didn't want to intrude, but I was filled with giddy gladness to be so close to two people who were in this one unrepeatable moment in life. I stared into my coffee, listening to them map out going to her mother's house to spread the news, and next to his cousins.... I beckoned the waiter and whispered, "Please, you've got to let me get their champagne." He smiled, his eyes twinkling. Later, when I signed the bill, there was no coffee charge on it. When I pointed that out, he said softly, "You got theirs. I got yours." In the moment, this struck me as the kindest thing ever.

Walking back to the subway, I replayed in my mind this small human chain: two people committing to love each other forever. Their joy inspiring me to buy them champagne. That gesture inspiring the waiter to give me my coffee. All of us in a fleeting spell of joy with one another.

Three years later, Bill and I were in Boulder, on our

drive home from O'Neill, Nebraska, where we'd attended the funeral service for John, Bill's father. We were taking a few days to regroup before finishing our drive back to Los Angeles. Bill had gone to CU Boulder back in the long-hair days of the seventies. We were having dinner with two of his old college friends, Tim and Sue, on the terrace of the historic Chautauqua meeting house. There are only a few Chautauquas left, and the one in Boulder is marvelous. Sprinkled all across America from about the 1880s on, they were summer camps for adults that brought learning and culture to the people. We watched the sun strike the Flatirons, the massive red rock peaks that jut out of the base of the Rockies. We basked in the twilight of the longest day of the year. It was nearly ten o'clock, and the air was still warm. Lots of wine. Stars began appearing.

"How far is the Cabrini Shrine from here?" I asked Tim, who'd lived in Boulder for forty-five years.

"Only about an hour south. A pretty drive," Tim said.

Bill shook his head, a silent no. "But honey, you go," he offered. "Tim and I will go look at cars."

The next day I headed from Boulder to Highway 40, out of Denver and up, up into the steep Rockies. It felt like I was gassing my Subaru to the top of the world. I turned in at the sign: "Welcome to Cabrini Shrine. Bearer of the Light of Jesus' Heart to the World." Adjacent was the sign that added, "No Skateboarding." The shrine comprises several sites on a big mountaintop, connected by blacktop parking lots and pathways. A chapel and gift store. Picnic areas. A rosary hike. A Stations of the Cross hike. A stone house. A tiny museum. A grotto with a spring of fresh running water. Big, big views of blue-green mountaintop after blue-green mountaintop. *Well*, I thought, a little befuddled by the altitude, *let's start in the gift shop*. Always a good place to kick off a prayerful experience....

The nice lady behind the counter, Joanne, sold me the souvenirs I'd selected: hand lotion made in Lourdes (rose scented!) and lots of little books like *Praying the Jesus Prayer*, which Christians have been saying for 1,900 years. I asked Joanne, who was all efficiency at the cash register, what she liked about working there. She smiled. "I've worked here twenty-seven years. I just love to see how much people enjoy themselves. They come for the quiet, for a break from life. A lot of personal healing happens here. People can feel it." She looked at me. She was taking a tiny break right now. But soon a long line of others was waiting.

Mother Cabrini purchased this mountaintop in 1900 to create a summer camp for her girls' orphanage in Denver. Today, in the shade, a teen youth group was unpacking sack lunches. The museum seemed like the next stop for me. It had the saint's bed and her writing desk. Another pair of tiny, pointy black shoes. And another curious grouping in a display case: her passport case, a bar of soap, a shoehorn. No sign said I couldn't sit at her desk. I was alone. I dared myself to sit in her place. It was nothing more than a youth-size rolltop desk with ten pigeonholes and a simple spindle-back chair. If I saw this desk at a yard sale I wouldn't give thirty bucks for it. But I felt audacious, even outrageous, sitting in her chair and pretending to be capable of the things she did. I could feel all the business, finance, entrepreneurship, plans, and correspondence materializing from her mind as she, too, would have sat there.

St. Frances Xavier Cabrini had no training in business, yet she bought and sold tracts of land, houses, hotels, and public buildings in New York, Chicago, Denver, New Orleans, Seattle, and Los Angeles, as well as in Italy, Nicaragua, and Argentina. A real estate tycoon! This was practically an impossibility for a woman in those days. Her feisty personality and the moral righteousness of her projects drew support from bishops, civic fathers, and wealthy Catholics. She was constantly on the alert for being cheated and for the good deal. Some called Mother Cabrini God's gypsy. She crossed the Atlantic back to Italy almost every year to report to Pope Leo XIII and to bring more sisters to America.

She built her first hospital in lower Manhattan because no one would treat the sick Italians when they arrived. She built her hospital in Chicago because no one wanted to treat all the dirty Italians working in the meat industry. She built her orphanage in Denver because there were so many Italians working the dangerous mines up in the Rockies, resulting in Italian orphans living on the streets of Denver. Mother Cabrini didn't care what nationality a poor or displaced person was. She saw herself, and the many young women she drew into her Missionary Sisters of the Sacred Heart, as "fragile vessels afloat in the world," tasked with bringing God's healing love to all. Because of this, she is the patron saint of all immigrants.

In 1905, after her years in Colorado, Mother Cabrini headed to Los Angeles. Bishop Conaty and the city's Catholics were by now aware of her abilities. They welcomed her with a Mass at St. Vibiana's Cathedral, a ride on the Red Car trolley, and a trip on a glass-bottom boat in Catalina. She used the publicity to help secure the donation of a mansion from the J.W. Robinsons, a department store family. She turned the mansion into Regina Coeli, the first orphanage for girls in Los Angeles (now the site of the Music Center). Mother Cabrini was spotted all over LA in her dilapidated horse and buggy, wearing a big straw hat over her tight wimple, scavenging used lumber from a defunct amusement park and befriending street children to help her. If the children she encountered were too sickly to help, she'd administer her own herb concoctions. She believed every girls' orphanage needed an attached industrial school to teach sewing, home arts, and bookkeeping, so her orphans could earn a living. This was an innovation for the time, when orphans were turned out at age twelve with no job training.

Still a real estate tycoon, she also set her eyes on 120 acres northeast of Los Angeles for her preventorium for girls at risk of TB, which later became Villa Cabrini Academy for girls and was sold in 1977 to Woodbury University. Mother Cabrini built the first buildings in what is today the city of Burbank, home to Disney Studios. A small shrine honoring the saint still exists in Burbank, now attached to St. Francis Xavier Church.

The idea of a saint actually walking and working in my own hometown was so startling that I couldn't sit at her desk on this Colorado mountainside any longer. I jumped up and hurried out of the museum. Feelings of weakness and selfishness filled me: I've been given health, intelligence, prosperity, and free time. What did it amount to in *me*? Snack mom for ten years of soccer games. Carpool driver. A helper where help is needed. A wife. A mother. A friend. An avid gift giver from yard-sale finds. It felt like such a small hill of beans.

Well, I thought, taking a big breath of clear air, *let's see what the spring is all about*. I strolled the meandering path to the spot where Mother Cabrini had thrown down her cane and told her sisters to dig, saying, "Here you will find water in this dry place." Fresh, sweet water has been springing from this improbable spot ever since—another hard-to-believe fun fact from the life of a lady saint. The spring feeds a big stainless-steel trough with water faucets so visitors can fill their water bottles or wash their faces.

The youth group had finished lunch and was here. A handsome Latina woman asked her charges, checking her cheat sheet, "What does it mean to go to the well? What was Jesus saying to the woman who met him at the well?" There was a long, long stretch of silence from the teens, so their chaperone assisted. "Yes, you are cleansed...forgiven. What does it mean to drink of the living waters?" Another long, long stretch of silence, and she assisted again, "Yes...you take in Christ's love." After a few more spoon-fed answers, and after jostling each other to get wet at the faucets, the kids bolted up the path. I was glad for them, despite their apparent lack of interest, because they had adults who cared enough to bring them here. And they will remember it, just as I remember my Girl Scout leaders and babysitters.

I said half a rosary with Bill in mind, hoping that he could share with me some of these little spiritual adventures I was taking, hoping as well that with his dad's passing, he wouldn't be left with too much undone father-son business.

Storm clouds were coming. The weather can change

so swiftly up in the mountains, and I was already wet in the two minutes it took to hurry to the car.

I saw a news item a couple of years ago that, due to overwhelming debt, Mother Cabrini High School in New York was closing after 117 years. Almost all of the students were scholarship students. My heart broke to think of the loss of opportunity for them. Was there no sports figure or startup mogul to come up with $7 million to keep this door open for these girls? Mother Cabrini's body, however, remained in the chapel, offering a bizarre and inspiring glimpse into the life of this woman who insisted, "I've done nothing. God's done everything."

Well, in my life I feel like I've got the *I've done nothing* part down. But the God part—do you just wait for Him to step into your shoes and hands and face and hair, like He's wearing a party costume? So He can walk around setting things right? We all find ways to be of help to one another, to set things a bit more right. That's our job in life. As my girls worked their way through high school, I became one of the theater moms who zipped everyone up and unsnarled hair for opening nights. My heart took me to teaching poetry very seriously, just around my kitchen table, to ten-year-olds so they might learn to love it, too. But Cabrini's like Paul Bunyan compared to that, walking across America one giant step at a time, crushing social dysfunction. It's ridiculous to compare any of our lives against that of a saint. But it's also true that we can each work with what we've got.

I wish Mother Cabrini were alive today, because as I learned about her, it made me wonder, what *would* she do about the homeless? What *would* she do about our neglected children? For that matter, what would St. Catherine of Siena, with her genius letter writing, do about the politicians in Washington? But St. Cabrini and St. Catherine are not alive today. It's just us regular folk. Spending time with Mother Cabrini made me realize that just because we're regular folk doesn't mean we're off the hook. We each have to work with whatever we have, in the way we have it.

"Women, like men, should try to do the impossible. And when they fail, their failure should be a challenge to others."

— AMELIA EARHART

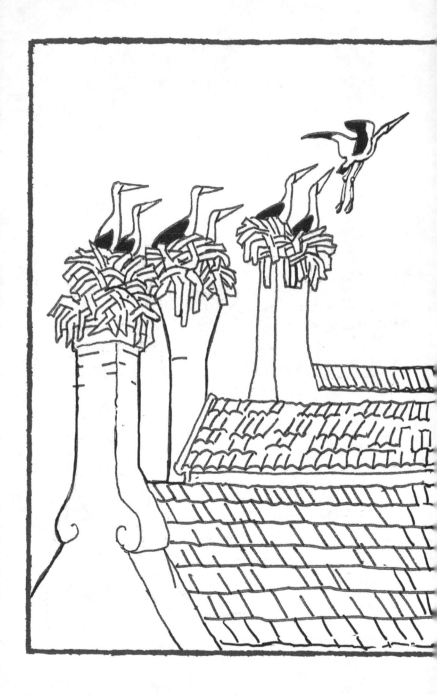

Four

Well, Not a Saint – A Statue

INFANT JESUS OF PRAGUE
16th century–present
Prague

Honestly, coffee helps. We began by drinking a Viennese coffee in the Café Louvre, a Belle Époque café in Prague, where waiters in starched aprons served coffee drinks piled high with cream. The gilded mirrors and copper ceiling transported us into the elegance of old middle Europe before the World Wars, and we planned our day.

It was 2009, and Bill and I were in the Czech capital to pick up Glennie, who'd just finished a semester abroad with the University of Richmond. Grace was done with her first year in faraway (for us) Iowa at Grinnell, and Rosie, now fifteen, was still at home—but for how long? Bill and I love our daughters so much, and their presence has hugely helped us put up with one another. After twenty-plus years together, we were really getting to live the phrase, "Marriage is work." Sometimes I'd look over the landscape of the years ahead and think, *Oh my gosh...what a desert...what will we do with each other?*

Anyway, in a burst of exuberance, we brainstormed this European trip. After all, we figured, it might be our last family trip before we lose the girls forever. I'd spontaneously tacked on a two-week program of immersion Spanish in Spain with just Rosie, wanting to hold her close before she'd be gone. But I was swamped with uncertainty.

I was in my late fifties. I worried that I was too old, too exhausted—from kids, and from helping Bill and sick parents who, of course, had died—and that maybe I was losing my own health. Where were the energy and imagination to discover the intrigue of an old city? Where was the stamina for the museums, for *the thousands of flights of steps* one takes when scrambling around Europe?

Plus, a new thing was happening. Random anxiety was blowing up in me on a moment's notice. A growing list of absurd worries kept leaping into my formerly happy, placid mind: *Oh God—I could fall down a hole—or break a tooth—or get dragged out by a wave—or what if the girls get kidnapped—what if the ransom is too high—what if the plane explodes—what what what if?!?*

Coffee done, we hopped onto a 1920s-era tram to ride through Malá Strana (Prague's Little City) and up to Prague Castle, everyone having fun because there we were all together—Bill, Grace, Glennie, Rose, and me—rollicking along. We passed the monument to the tragedy of the Communist Era. We passed all the busy shops with their vintage canvas awnings. We passed a church with its courtyard full of people. "What's going on there?" I asked Glennie, our expert.

"Mom, it's the weirdest thing. It's the Infant Baby Jesus of Prague in there. They have a baby doll dressed up in gold clothes and people come from *everywhere* to see it. It's supposed to be miraculous."

"Have you gone?"

"No!" she said, reminding me in a word of her current level of interest in religion.

"I want to see it," I said. "Come on, let's go."

"But we're going to the castle," Bill said.

"Come on everyone, come with me. Let's do this instead." Each said, no, no, and no—no one wanted to stop and see a miraculous baby Jesus statue. The tram trundled right past the church.

But then the tram stopped at a stoplight and Rosie turned to me and said, "Okay, Mom, I'll go with you," and in a spontaneous moment, we hopped off and waved goodbye to the others.

Our Lady of Victory Church was as gloomy as 600 years of Prague's history. And indeed, high on a gold altar, in an ornate glass case, perched a six-teenth-century doll, a wooden and wax likeness—sort of—of baby Jesus. The child held an orb in one hand, his fingers of the other hand posed in a gesture of blessing. The baby was dressed top to bottom in golden brocade, crowned in gold, too. Maybe seventy-five people were praying around the Infant Jesus, or the Baby Child, or is it the Child Baby of Prague? The gloom and the gold were too much for even me, and I was thinking, *How can we get out of here and go to the castle and find our family?* But this was a UNESCO World Heritage Site that attracts people from around the world who want to offer prayers, submit requests, and receive blessings. So we stayed.

We ventured into the gift shop, which was stuffed with all things baby Jesus, all the time: calendars, statues, keychains, plaques, tea towels, almost all of them referencing a particular prayer, the novena to the Infant Jesus of Prague. In the Catholic world there are various types of novenas, but basically, they're all a prayer repeated daily for nine straight days, requesting or giving thanks for something, either spiritual or worldly. I flipped through a hefty five-pound gift book. It explained how, since the sixteenth century when the small statue arrived in Prague from Spain as a wedding gift to the new queen, Maria Manriquez de Lara, it has been credited with all types of miracles: restoring health, granting wealth, protection from the Nazis, you name it.

When one prays in the presence of the statue, or prays this particular novena, one is told to expect good things to flow. On the last page of the picture book was a copy of this famous novena. *I love it—they have a speedy version!* If you need that miracle quick, just say the novena for nine consecutive hours, instead of days, to get your request answered.

Taking a pen and a paper napkin from my purse, I quickly copied the novena down. Maybe sometime later, if I felt like it, I'd have a look.

Jet ahead three weeks. Every day had been an inward trial but an outward glory. Vienna, Venice, and Paris are such fabulous cities, but, as I overshared earlier, much of my thinking was taken up with, *Shit, it's so hot and my clothes are so tight.... Crap, Bill's grumpy again.... Hey, those people cut in line over there.... Is our waiter dissing us?... That policeman is looking at me!*

After Paris, Bill, Glennie, and Grace headed for home, and Rosie and I took a quick flight to Madrid and then a four-hour van ride across the wide plain of La Mancha to the medieval city of Salamanca. Two weeks of immersion Spanish: She'd be in a summer camp with other fifteen-year-olds living with various host families, and me? I rented what turned out to be a back bedroom from a creaky old Spanish couple who made a few bucks by taking in students. Actually, the "bedroom" was their storage room—in went the extra dining room set, in went the portable wardrobe stuffed with clothes they never wore, in went the broken TV, and in went the crazy lady from Pasadena who thought this would all be fun. They watched soccer and sensational newscasts all day and all night. How many times could one watch the Pamplona news cameras zoom in on the trampled boy? The ten-car pileup in the Alps? The train derailment in Toulouse? And they watched all this quality TV in darkness. They had a meter on the light switches, a meter on the hot water taps, and they grumbled if the light was ever on in my room.

Not quite the fun international couple I'd pictured sitting and drinking wine with. But I lacked the energy to find a new place, so I just told myself to make the best of it. After morning Spanish class, which was turning out to be really dull, I'd wander around Salamanca alone, looking at ancient stone walls and statues of conquistadors and worrying about Rosie. So many drunk American teenagers stumbled in and out of the bars—no drinking age here. The last I'd seen of my lovely fifteen-year-old was when she and I met Marta, her *new* mother, in a café. Suddenly I was chopped liver. Even though Marta was my age, in the wintertime she worked as a fur-coat model in stores. Come summertime, she laid by her pool, did her nails, and took in students. Marta wore blue eyeliner, and her hair was a bright, flowing, damaged blond. Rosie couldn't *wait* to jump in her car and be off. This stupid arrangement had seemed clever when I planned it—Rosie having her adventure in a foreign city and me having mine, without me hovering over her. But now it just threw gasoline on my anxieties.

One day I found myself sitting on a bench in the shade in front of St. Esteban's church. I'd been staring up at the stork nests wedged in the high towers—three nests, each the size of a great big wicker laundry basket. I watched the giant birds come and go from their marvelous homes. I wondered if the nests could be blown away by the wind. If so, would the eggs splatter all over the plaza? Would people slip on the shattered eggs? That would hurt so much! Would they slip hard enough to break a leg? Would anyone help them? They'd be lying there crying! *What the heck was I doing in this city? And the beggars! Beggar women and children crying out, "Ayuda me—ayuda me!" They jumped up and chased after the tourists—beating their breasts, hobbling on deformed feet—ohhh, what was I doing here?* Everyone and everything, even the sun, so hot but so beautifully pale on the stone buildings, seemed cold, ominous. I had at least another week of this "vacation." Get me outta here!

I thought of that folded-up napkin in my purse. I was literally doing nothing but sitting there, letting myself spin out of control. The instructions for the novena were to think of an important request, an urgent situation you have. Fix the exact wording in your mind, and when you think you really know what your prayer is for, pray it with all your might, with the full force of your being. Pray it like you mean it so, so much.

Okay, I thought, I need and want better mental health. I need and want better physical vitality. *Please*—help me deal with all the football-basketball-hockey-baseball-Tour-de-France that dominates our home life, that Bill loves but that leaves me cold. What about my completely fallow creativity? I'm too insecure to even say I want to get back to writing. *Pick a request, Mary Lea—shoot, why not give all of it to Him right now?* I put all of my requests—mental health, physical health, marriage health, and personal creativity—into the novena to the Infant Jesus of Prague all at once and sat on that bench and prayed as hard as I could.

The instant I completed the prayer, a relief—a betterment—came over me. It was small but real. The jolt of positivity was memorable because it was so instant. I looked around the plaza. The ladies walking arm in arm, the man standing in front of his trinket shop—it all seemed very pleasant. The sun was beautiful on the stone walls, not threatening. Those stork nests had been up in the towers for as long as any shopkeeper remembered. "Forever," one said to me. "Nothing can bother them." Taking my situation seriously, I thought, *Let's see about that speedy version of the novena.* I decided that for the next eight hours, on the hour, I would repeat the prayer, bringing to it all the intensity and earnestness I could, and I'd see what happens.

What happened? The crazy, random anxiety went away. A helpful energy filled me, encouraging me to care for myself: eat better, drink less, show myself a little compassion. Each time I gave myself over to the prayer, the benefit was instantaneous. After that day, I didn't stop. I said that prayer as my morning ritual for several years. I'd change the requests every nine days or repeat them if the need hadn't been met yet. I made requests like: help Brigid afford a house—save Mark's life—get Kevin well employed—guide Bill's business decisions—protect our daughters, for they are far away, in the friends they attract, their romantic situations, their employment. Many of those requests were met, and I believe that happened with help from this prayer. But mostly I pray for myself, asking that energy and wellness continually flood me so that I can be and do what I want in life. And for Bill and me, that we can appreciate each other despite our differences. I can't prove that the successes are because of the Infant Child of Prague, the curious waxen image of baby Jesus, but prayer is prayer. Amazingly, even Bill, ever the skeptic, will say to me when faced with a life problem, "Mary Lea, get the baby Jesus of Prague going."

In seeking out lady saints and in spending the

time on my own spirit life, I've come to learn three things about prayers of request:

One: You must be very specific in what you pray for.

Two: You have to really, deeply want it.

Three: You must pray with the total intensity of your being, as if your very life depended on it. Focusing your mind in this way brings the loving power of the universe to the cause at hand.

For the remaining seven days in Salamanca, I busied myself with following the stars and seashells embedded in the sidewalks that lead pilgrims who are on the Camino de Santiago. People come from all over the world to walk this 500-mile medieval path, which starts in France and ends in Santiago de Compostela. How thrilled I was to realize that Salamanca was on the route! I spoke to pilgrims resting their feet, and I rested my feet with them. I toured the third-oldest university in Europe, where students literally sat at the feet of their teachers. I took a bus to Segovia to see the Roman aqueduct, and another to Avila to see St. Teresa of Avila's bedroom and convent. The heat was so intense in Avila that I couldn't have the experience I'd hoped for, but it still lit a fire of curiosity that I returned to years later.

I bought a notebook and commenced writing every day. Writing about the street life at night, where entire families promenade around the plaza, nipping into tapas bars and lingering over street musicians. Writing about the strangeness of coming from California, where every city has a Portola or a Cortes or a Cabrillo street, to Salamanca, where every street has a Portola or Cortes or Cabrillo statue, honoring men who conquered California for the glory of Spain. I wrote about the weirdness of the Salamanca beggars, who sit by the fountains performing a horrendous performance art, actually beating on their breasts, yelling and begging to heaven for alms, in contrast to our passive beggars at freeway exits.

Before I knew it, it was time to collect Rosie and head for home. She'd had the time of her life hanging out with kids from Switzerland, Brazil, Israel, and the UK, watching bootlegged movies, eating squid, and staying out late. I was calm when Marta zoomed into the bus station with only five minutes to spare before the only bus to the airport was to leave. There was a hopefulness in me that I knew was coming from my spirit. I had begun to take care of my spirit, and in the future, I would try to protect it from becoming so malnourished.

The trip to Prague and Salamanca was nine years ago. We all know how one thing always leads to another. Through saying this prayer, the idea of writing this book about the lady saints came to me. So thank you, baby Jesus.

Novena to the Infant Jesus of Prague

Oh Jesus who has said, ask and ye shall receive. Seek and ye shall find. Knock and the door shall be opened. Through the intercession of Mary, your most Holy Mother, I request **(insert your request here)**

Oh Jesus who has said, all that you ask of the Father in my name, He will grant you. Through the intercession of Mary, your most Holy Mother, I urgently request **(repeat your request here)**

Oh Jesus, who has said, the earth shall pass away, but my word shall not pass away. Through the intercession of Mary, your most Holy Mother, I am confident my request is granted **(repeat your request here)**

Then finish with this short closing prayer:

Divine Infant Jesus, I know you love me and would never leave me. I thank you for your close presence in my life and I believe in your promise of peace, blessing, and freedom from want.

Amen

Enjoy your life.

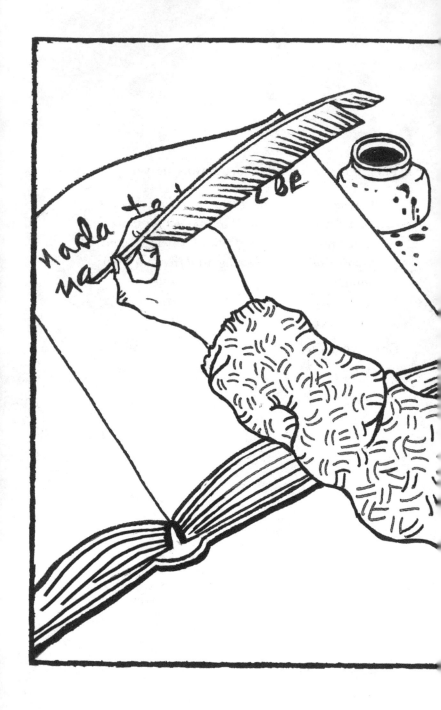

Five

Doctor! Doctor!

St. Teresa of Avila
1515–1582
Avila, Spain, and Rome, Italy

While in Salamanca, a sign in a tourist window caught my eye: DAY TRIP TO AVILA. Avila had not been on my radar, but here it was, available on a platter. A chance to see another saint! And so cheap: $29 for the day. I could just hop right on the bus.

The full bus took off with the tour guide hissing and lisping the true Spanish dialect into the mic. *Oh, gosh,* I knew right away, *it'd be a whole day of not understanding a word.* Why hadn't I recognized my limits and opted for the slightly more expensive English guide? Soon the air conditioning broke, making the man next to me fall fast asleep, his head bobbing on my shoulder. It was only ten in the morning. The guide lisped on and on like he'd been doing this tour

24/7 for 500 years. The $29 faded out as any kind of bargain. You get what you pay for.

The open countryside leading up to Avila is so stark and so hot in August that the medieval fortress walls appeared shimmering and mirage-like. They say Avila is the finest example of a walled city anywhere in the world, with crenelated gun towers, battlements, and arched gates, all the glory of eleventh-century solidness. *Those Moors'll never get us!*

Our guide led us through the gates and gave us the options: a climb on the walls, a visit to the convent of St. Teresa, or going for ice cream. Most of the group followed him directly to ice cream, and I peeled off for two hours to do what I wanted in this magnificently preserved UNESCO World Heritage city.

The center for all things Teresa is the church, built over the house in which she was born in 1515. The church is attached to her former convent, and in the underground crypt, which was hers, there's a little museum. It was built in 1636, soon after her swift canonization. People already recognized her as a saint even before she died, because of her remarkable talents and achievements.

I strode across the baking stone plaza to reach it. On view are her wooden block pillow (ouch), her spinning wheel, and examples of her famous swervy penmanship and exquisite embroidery. But between the heat and the glare, as sharp as twisted tinfoil,

I felt cranky and annoyed. Not taking the time to read all the literature made me miss her relic high above the church altar—weirdly, truly, it is her once-pumping, now-shriveled heart! How could I have missed that? What I mostly remember of my visit was the display case showing her scourge, which she administered to herself three times a week, and her—pretty funky but *not* totally decayed—finger adorned with a mesmerizing square-cut emerald ring. For me: a scourge, no; an emerald, yes.

Really, most of my exploration time was spent finding shade and losing myself in the lovely, clean, buff-colored stone ramparts, stone streets, and stone steps. Find some shade, find some coffee, and lose myself in the lure of past centuries.

Ten years after that day in Avila, I could still picture the cool, clear green of that emerald. And now, all these years later, I wanted to know more. I wanted to know about the only other woman (besides Catherine of Siena) in 2,000 years to be declared a Doctor of the Church. (Two more women in this new millennium, Thérèse of Lisieux and Hildegard of Bingen, have joined the club.) A woman so filled with zeal, so impatient with mediocracy that she went up against the Inquisition, and so willing to demand more of herself that her influence has flowed down the centuries. So I did my homework to learn more about the saint who had intrigued me ever since that sweltering day in Spain.

Like the other women I've met who became superheroes for the centuries, St. Teresa didn't start out that way. She became that way, one day at a time.

She was born Teresa Sanchez de Cepeda. Her father, Alonso, was a wealthy wool merchant in Avila. His father had been a Marrano, meaning a Jew forced to convert to Christianity. This was a dark event in Spanish history. Alonso, in fact, bought himself a knighthood so his assimilation would be without question in strict Spanish society. Thus, Teresa was an aristocrat—and not just that, but also one of the great beauties of Avila. She could have had any husband she wanted. This was the Spain of global domination: Castilla y Leon, seat to Ferdinand and Isabella, underwriters of the new world—riches were pouring in from the Americas and Asia. Avila, Segovia, and Salamanca were powerhouse cities of northern Spain, suppressors of the Moors and leaders of the high Spanish Renaissance. It was a truly dizzying period of world history.

There are accounts of how Teresa had three charming dimples and magnificent black hair. Writers of the time noted her laughter, her socializing, and her enjoyment of life. But she did not want to marry. She couldn't abide the idea of spending her life having baby after baby, being bossed around by a husband, and not being allowed to have her own opinion. She knew, however, how easily she could be led into worldly sin. It is said that she and St. Francis of Assisi had the same problem: They both suffered from such an abundance of charm and attraction that they had more friendships than could be handled. So if she wouldn't marry, she had to enter the convent. Those were her two choices. Don't want to marry? Off you go. Her father begged her to marry, but she was stubborn. She selected the Carmelite convent.

Carmelites today are nuns and friars who dedicate themselves to praying and improving the world through a life of contemplation and prayer, often in seclusion. The order reaches all the way back to the Old Testament, with the prophet Elijah and his mysticism at Mt. Carmel, thousands and thousands of years ago. Carmelites came to Europe when some pilgrims traveled with the crusaders to the Holy Land and discovered the beauty of the valleys around Mt. Carmel. These pilgrims set themselves up as hermits. Eventually, the Muslims asked them in no uncertain terms to leave, and they fled with their lives back to Europe, taking their spirituality with them.

So many young women were in Teresa's boat— prosperous and educated but wanting to escape marriage—that convents at that time were surprisingly worldly and social places. Women had more freedoms there than in family structures. They could bring their wealth. Parlors were decorated with generous gifts from relatives. There were dinner parties. Some nuns wore jewelry and colorful scarves. Despite these distractions, through contemplation and prayer, depths began to open for Teresa. She began studying from *The Third Alphabet*, a popular mystical text at the time that explained that friendship with God in this life is possible by cleansing one's conscience, resting in loving stillness, and then rising up to God alone. She read and re-read it, the way she had devoured romance novels in secret when younger.

Increasingly, Teresa sought her inner space, going into what she later dubbed in her writings "mental prayer," a form of intense spiritual self-concentration. Eastern religions have often been dominated by spiritual mysticism, but not so much in the West, so this was unusual.

It seems to me that "spiritual self-concentration" is another way of saying "take a look at your soul"—a means of going into dialogue with yourself. Ask yourself if you're on the right path. Are you doing what the little voice inside says? Try talking to yourself this directly—it's hard. St. Teresa also called it self-knowledge, and she said that one day of self-knowledge was worth three days of prayer. Instantly, she advanced our understanding of the complexities of being human.

Through her focus and mental prayers, a fierce love of God bloomed in her. Increasingly, the shallowness and lack of spiritual growth in her community began to trouble her. She could go for days in total silent devotion. She would retreat, seeming to be asleep, but in fact she was in a deep state of trance, her heart and mind on fire in communication with God.

In her twenties she began to receive what she called "favors" and "treats": raptures, levitations, and visions that became an everyday part of her life. Reportedly, she was sometimes completely suspended in the air for an entire Mass. Obviously, testaments of being suspended in the air are hard to believe, but I like being able to roll with it. Accounts of such mysteries dot all cultures and most religions. For instance, Buddha is often depicted as floating just off the ground. Teresa just must have had an awful lot of spiritual energy!

During this time, Teresa also rose to become a more and more powerful administrator of her convent. She could no longer tolerate the flaws in the community she now ran. The frivolousness and comforts. Her restlessness grew as she learned to easily move between the two worlds of contemplation and action. It was in one of her days-long raptures when God instructed her to write. She said to Him, "Why do you want me to write a prayer book? There are already so many! I'm unfit for it. I'm nothing but a stupid woman!" But she did begin to write, in great, long bouts of rapturous seclusion. What resulted was *My Life*, which the Inquisition picked apart for being "too personal." Who was *she* to write so personally about God? Then came *The Way to Perfection*, and then her masterpiece, *The Interior Castle*.

I ordered *The Interior Castle* online, and two days later, a nifty blue paperback arrived in my mailbox, 441 years after she wrote it.

I opened it, afraid I couldn't handle something written so long ago. I have never been a strong reader, and sure enough, it wasn't easy to navigate. Teresa's heavy with the "I am wicked and ashamed" stuff, so typical of spiritual development in the sixteenth century, but she was amazingly clear in describing the steps to developing one's mysticism, the "fleeing of the senses," the delectable sweetness of it, the travel one takes in moving from one interior room to the next for spiritual growth. Her writings, and particularly this book, are what earned her the title of Doctor of the Church for their contributions in humankind's quest for self-understanding. Freud drew from this book when developing his theories. It's compared to Buddha's Eightfold Path to Nirvana. She wrote it in 1577.

I felt virtuous, working my way through the book while going about my daily duties: getting the oil changed in the Subaru, finishing up the details after Grace's garden wedding, keeping up with emails. It's fun to read something ancient while doing something modern.

To get to know Teresa more, I copied out a list of her most engaging quotes and carried it around with me, tucked in my purse or open on the seat of my car while running errands. It turned out to be so helpful! For instance, this year, to my great aggrievement, I had to appear *in person* at the Department of Motor Vehicles. Is there no worse torture than having to show up at the DMV? Hours of your life you'll never get back, but Teresa made me laugh right out loud in line—after I'd been told to stand there, get a number here, wait over yonder, oops, go to the computers, tell us everything again, now get your number. I glanced at my quote sheet only to see: "No pain is permanent." No pain is permanent, even if it involves the DMV. Good one, Teresa!

And a quote I didn't know was attributed to her:

> *God has no hands on earth but yours,*
> *No feet on earth but yours*
> *No eyes of compassion on earth but yours*

I find this one utterly compelling. She is saying that *we* are supposed to act like God would, in the care of one another.

Teresa's dive into a deeper union with God gave her the confidence to deal with the decay of the entire Carmelite order, which it (and the Church in general) had been experiencing for more than a hundred years. This was the dawn of the Counter-Reformation, when the Church began correcting its corrupt ways. A large chunk of Catholics had already broken away as part of the Protestant Reformation, because they just couldn't take the decay of values anymore. It was during this time that Teresa began a physically stringent, spiritually rigorous break-away branch of her order, which she called the Discalced Carmelites, or Without-Shoes Carmelites. They were also without rich food, without wealth and ownership, without the many, many distractions that keep us from spiritual growth.

For the next twenty years, until the end of her life, Teresa traveled every corner of Spain by foot and rocky donkey path, setting up monasteries and convents for those called to deeply, contemplatively experience God. The old fun-loving Carmelites didn't like how popular her movement swiftly became, and because of that, Teresa was under house arrest for three years and faced harassment from the Inquisition. She was not physically tortured, but friends of hers were, notably John of the Cross, her partner reformer for the friars. It was not until she was able to personally, eloquently plead her case before King Philip II that the persecutions stopped. Today, she's acknowledged as the reformer of the Carmelites, and she is the patron saint of Spain.

It's a testament to St. Teresa's remarkable mind that not only was she capable of rapturous contemplation, but she was also quite witty. One account tells of a stormy night when she and two of her nun companions, dealing with stubborn donkeys, finally arrived at a friend's lodging in the pouring rain. Drenched and shivering, they stood outside knocking and waiting for the door to open. She looked up to heaven and called out, "If this is how you treat your friends, it's no wonder you have so few!"

One afternoon, her quote, "Be gentle with others and stern with yourself," came up from the bottom of my purse while I was searching for my wallet at the supermarket. Again, it made me laugh, because who wouldn't rather be easy on herself and stern with others? I've actually been taking all her quotes to heart, what with attempting to read *The Interior Castle*. It encourages my own self-examination. As little kids in Catholic school, we learned to "examine our consciences" on Friday afternoons and then go to confession as a class. My confessed sins were typically something like: I coveted someone else's candy. Or I took my sister's Halloween candy because she wouldn't eat it fast enough. Or I watched as my cousin shoplifted candy because no one was looking. Sometimes I couldn't think of anything to confess, so I'd make up something like: I lied to my mother. Soul-searching at its finest.

My confession practice fell by the wayside over the decades because I consider myself a good person. Today, I sort of go to the gym instead. Hold myself to a size-twelve pant and don't eat sugar. Obviously,

obviously, obviously it's not the same. I just *want* it to be. But it's so hard to think about parsing out a real response toward homelessness, or my desire to shop and acquire when I already have so much. This crazy little blue paperback seemed to be calling me out.

Relics have always been a thing in the Catholic church. It's compelling to be so close to a piece of a person who was once so important. I mean, wouldn't it be fun to try on Marilyn Monroe's shoes? To sleep in Abraham Lincoln's bed in the White House? For believers, relics are a way to see that the saints once were real and the stories were true. Of course, the Church has preserved relics of St. Teresa of Avila. There is quite a story about her hand:

During the Spanish Civil War, many churches were assaulted by anticlerical forces. St. Teresa's left hand, encased in a gem-encrusted silver glove with strategic peepholes to see her fingerbones, was stolen from the Carmelite nuns in Ronda when their convent was looted. When the "national side" took the city of Ronda back, they found piles of priceless valuables from the churches, St. Teresa's hand among them. General Franco asked officials if he could take it—he did, and he kept it until he died! For forty years it was in the possession of Spain's authoritarian ruler, accompanying him on his travels, and it sat by his deathbed in 1975. Only then did the Carmelites get it back. Today it rests in a darkened room under lock and key and under their watch. They bring it out for special veneration.

Another thing, not as bizarre, but to me amazing, given my interests, is that legend has it—legend going back to before 1700—that she, Teresa of Avila, was the first to have the Infant Child of Prague! The elaborate statue of the baby Jesus was given to her and her convent by wealthy supporters. She and her nuns enjoyed changing its clothes, the way a mother would change her baby. Until Teresa divested herself of most worldly possessions, she traveled with it. She felt it offered her protection. *She's* the one who gave it to Maria Manriquez de Lara as a gift when Maria was departing to become the new queen of Bohemia. Legend says that St. Teresa told Maria to keep the statue where she could see it, pray to Jesus, and her wants and cares would be taken care of. Just like today! This is too strange for me to believe, but the Infant Child of Prague is officially in the care of the Carmelites of Prague, as it has been for some 400 years, when it was given back to them by the royal family of Bohemia.

Earlier this year, I visited Rome. What a playground for all things saints!

It was pure luck to get a fellow named Gregory as a guide for my excursion to the catacombs. His expertise is early Christian history. When traveling alone, being curious and outgoing is so helpful. Meeting a person like Gregory can make your trip. He accepted my invitation for a coffee, a drink, a crab salad—whatever it would take to have him sit down with me for a bit after the tour. His encyclopedic mind was a treasure trove. In a sidewalk café, we ordered Aperol spritzes, the fizzy late afternoon drink of Italian choice. He told me that St. Catherine of Siena's head was definitely not in Rome. "No, no, definitely no. Whoever told you it was on loan for 300 years didn't know anything. It's there, you just missed it," he said, speaking in a way nerdy, super-brilliant people speak.

"Oh," I said. After a little pause, "What do you know about Teresa of Avila?"

"You've been to Santa Maria della Vittoria?" he asked bluntly.

"No, not yet, but I've heard of the statue." He put his drink to his lips and drained it.

"Come on. I'll take you there." I paid and we left. After a short distance we found the church. It's a gilded jewel box inside. To the left of the altar, in its own marble stage setting, is the enormous, fantastic Bernini stone sculpture, *The Ecstasy of St. Teresa*. Gregory said it's arguably the greatest seventeenth-century stone sculpture in the world.

"Look how it seems to float. Look at the complexity of folds of cloth. Look at her expression!" he ordered. Between the beauty of her swooning form, the gilded rays pouring down, and the flight of the angel with the spear with which he will pierce her heart, it is a thing of wondrous beauty.

The event depicted in the statue reportedly actually happened to St. Teresa. In one notable rapture, an angel came down and pierced her heart again and again, causing great pain and extreme pleasure. "It's pretty spectacular isn't it?" Gregory asked. "Bernini was *the* Michelangelo after Michelangelo died." He then looked at his watch. "Oh, I gotta go." And he left.

About thirty people stood around staring at St. Teresa that Monday afternoon, me among them, feeling privileged to know as much as I did about her. Many other tourists cruised by, took a moment, and carried on in ignorance. I stayed quite a while, thinking about her.

St. Teresa died at age sixty-seven. By then, her teeth had turned black, hair grew from the three dimples, and her rocky, worn-out boots were still on her feet. What she died of is hard to know: uterine cancer or possibly TB or even a form of Lyme disease—something with crushing symptoms that came and went over much of her life. Her reformed Carmelites, starting with the seventeen monasteries and convents she personally founded, are worldwide today. It amazes me that right near me in Pasadena are both types of Carmelites, the cloistered and the social-action orders, who've been helping our world since 1919.

St. Teresa of Avila directly influenced Marie Francois-Martin, who became St. Teresa of Lisieux, and Anjeze Bojaxhiu of Albania, who became St. Mother Teresa of Calcutta. And here in Rome, via Bernini's white marble, stubborn St. Teresa from arid Spain ravishes all who come and see. She lives forever in her words, in her deeds, and in art.

A final word from St. Teresa of Avila

May you use those gifts that you have received, and pass on the love that has been given to you.

Six

A Is for Apple, B Is for Big Apple, S Is for Saint

St. Elizabeth Ann Seton
1774–1821
New York City

This time, searching for saints took me into the years I'm just glad to have survived—all those years in school.

My bare-bones Catholic schoolyard in Pasadena seemed like nothing but hot blacktop and bullies. The nuns showed only their faces, and I daydreamed endlessly out the window, wishing to be away from there. My prison years were 1958 to 1967, sitting obediently and quietly all day long, forty of us to a room. It's so painful for someone with ADD and dyslexia, mysterious afflictions labeled in those days under the blanket terms, *dumb* and *disorganized*. So when I said earlier that it was some karmic wheel I was on to send my own children to St. Elizabeth's,

I wasn't kidding. Happily, Catholic education has changed much in fifty-plus years.

My parents were determined to send all nine of us to Catholic school, and even though I flunked the third grade, I did, apparently, learn a few things. My father had long bouts of unemployment, followed by a bankruptcy after the failure of a car wash business he started, followed by long periods of unemployment again. But they scraped together the $85 per kid to pay tuition. My mother would take hot dogs and put them through a meat grinder and add a lot of mayonnaise and relish to make mystery-spread sandwiches, a dubious switch from peanut butter and jelly. She could take a very small can of tuna and dump so much mayonnaise into it that she'd get seven sandwiches out of it—voilà, years' worth of sack lunches. Even today the thought of my own elementary school years makes me feel anxious and inadequate.

Let it go, I thought as I rattled about in the back of a yellow cab speeding down the JFK highway, with a mental wave of the hand. It all worked out. The past is the past. I grew up just fine. Bill's businesses—he'd actually built two of them in Hollywood—have been prosperous. How lucky we were to be vacationing in New York City again on this crisp early Sunday morning in October, with those school years many decades behind me. The cab was taking me to the southern tip of Manhattan.

It was 2015, and New York was still buoyant after the first visit from Pope Francis, the new and exciting head of the church. I'd been glued to the TV at home, watching him ride up 5th Avenue, the crowds so huge I thought of when Liz Taylor rode into Rome on an elephant in *Cleopatra*. A joke, of course, because Francis is the opposite of opulent. That's what makes people crazy for him. He's the one who took a Syrian family to live with him at the Vatican. He's the one who did behind-the-scenes diplomacy between Cuba and the United States, thawing the freeze. He's the one who told rigid Catholics to stop obsessing over gays and lesbians and think other, more loving and merciful thoughts. I sat attentively on the couch, listening to his speech before Congress, the speech at which Joe Biden was crying. Pope Francis especially called out the names of four Americans who changed history: St. Mother Elizabeth Ann Seton, Martin Luther King Jr., Abraham Lincoln, and Dorothy Day.

Mother Elizabeth Ann Seton...I kind of knew about her. But I didn't know she was the first American-born saint. I didn't know she'd been a wealthy, beautiful socialite married to an import/export tycoon and had had five children. I didn't know she started the first parochial school, which means it's open to poor families, an innovation that would spread to educate up to four million American children annually during the height of the Baby Boom. I didn't know she was from New York. So I decided to go check out her shrine down by the Staten Island Ferry. It was so early on a Sunday morning that the crowds headed to the Statue of Liberty wouldn't be there yet.

Stepping out of the cab, I stood trying to take it all in: At this spot in Manhattan, the steel and glass office buildings are so crowded and vertical, the scale so gigantic, that I didn't even see the two tiny red-and-white buildings right across the street, looking like little buttons at the bottom of an upright crate of steel rods. But there they were: the Watson House, which is the oldest continually inhabited house in Manhattan, from 1793, and adjoining it, a prim brick church, Our Lady of the Rosary, which is Mother Seton's shrine and stands on the site of her home. I tried to imagine the area inhabited with brave little buildings like them, nothing over two or three stories, windows of hand-poured wavy glass, and each brick laid, of course, by hand. The New York when George Washington marched his troops down Wall Street. The New York with a harbor full of triple-decker merchant ships, frigates, cutters, and man-of-wars.

Elizabeth Ann Seton's family was among the earliest English Colonial settlers in New York. She was from the Episcopal aristocracy. A debutante, she married wealthy William Seton, who had a lucrative trade business to Italy with his merchant ships.

They lived in a fine house and were neighbors of Alexander Hamilton. Like all ladies of wealth, she did charity work, in her case focused on education. The only schools in New York (and most places) in those days were elite private schools for boys. Wealthy girls, after tutoring at home, attended music and culture-focused finishing schools. The poor and the middle class were out of luck when it came to education. This was a time when society made no provision for the ill, the imprisoned, the immigrants, the widowed, the orphaned, the poor, the lame, the uneducated. All of this was left to ladies of wealth, and reports state that Elizabeth thrived on and found joy in this work and in teaching her own five children at home, as well as William's six younger siblings, whom they'd taken in when William's father died. How surprising today to think society hadn't yet made any provisions for general education.

Well, Elizabeth's life took a pretty hard left turn. Their wealth began to evaporate due to piracy on the high seas. Her husband's health collapsed with the early signs of TB. They decided to sail to Italy and its warm weather to rescue his health, but when they arrived, they were mistakenly trapped in cold, murky, yellow-fever quarantine quarters for a month, and he died there. She then got word that their wealth had completely vanished, because so many of her husband's ships had been hit by piracy or attacked by the French. She was stranded in Italy. She had just turned twenty-nine. Her oldest daughter was with her, but the younger four children were in the charge of her sister-in-law back in New York.

Standing there, gazing at the huge, impersonal city around me, I realized that there's no way to truly understand how bad it got for her—and too, how fragile the good times might be for *any* of us. No matter how together or on top of things we might be, trouble can come for reasons we can't predict.

Widowed and stranded in Italy in 1803, Elizabeth and her daughter were taken in by the merchant Filippo Filicchi, who'd been a business associate of her husband's, and his American wife. The Filicchis were kind and generous. Elizabeth learned about Catholicism from them and had a profound spiritual awakening based primarily on Communion. She developed the feeling that the sacrament of Holy Communion was *truly* Jesus Christ, not a symbol of Jesus Christ. This is a significant difference between the Catholic and Episcopal faiths. She was awestruck by the act of taking Communion.

Thinking about her high, high level of spirituality fascinates me. I've never experienced anything remotely like this, but as I've learned about the lady saints, I've come to realize that they all developed a powerful desire and then ability to connect to God with every fiber of their being. I now think I can taste a tiny bit of how they felt as I watch my own spirituality steadily growing, the more I think and pray about things.

America was virulently anti-Catholic in Elizabeth's time. It was a bold and damning move on her part to convert. When she returned to New York a year later, the doors of society closed to her. Not only had her husband died, but so had her father-in-law and sister-in-law, so now she was solely responsible for the six younger brothers and sisters of her deceased husband. She began teaching to make ends meet, and she had to move to ever-cheaper housing because of her large brood.

For the next few years, Elizabeth taught in her home and attempted to start a girls' boarding school, but her existence was hand-to-mouth. Few people wanted a Catholic to educate their children. A debilitating emotional anxiety followed her. When she came upon the words to the Memorare, a prayer that has been cherished by Catholics since the twelfth century, it became a hook to hang her trust and confidence on. The Virgin Mary became her everything. Her prayer life and her emotional connection to the Eucharist became stronger, sustaining her through depressions, deaths of loved ones, and terrible uncertainty. A vision began to grow in her: Educate the poor so they could rise.

I'm not sure how long I'd been standing across from these two little buildings musing on these facts, but it was much later in the morning, and the area was crowded with tourists. People were flowing off the Staten Island Ferry. Young, skinny, hopeful immigrant African men were pestering everyone to buy Hop-On, Hop-Off Big Apple bus tickets. "See the sights! Come, Miss, come—empty seats now. Buy one! Hop on!" Others encouraged everyone to buy toy cars, fake designer watches, rubber duckies, and cheap hoodies. They hustled as hard as anyone could in worn-out flip-flops and old gym pants. With all the work that needs doing in this Land of the Free, why is this intense energy being used so pointlessly? *Don't let them fall through the cracks*, I prayed quietly as I refused every come-on. *They've gotten themselves here, America. Please give 'em a shot.*

Well, Elizabeth had determination and energy. She was also supposed to have been beautiful, so while her Catholicism closed many doors to her, her beauty and energy opened others. Ranking Catholics of the day introduced her around. There was only one Catholic bishop in America at this time, John Carroll of Baltimore. They had a chance meeting at the one and only Catholic church in New York, the Church of St. Peter, which is still there, just north of the World Trade Center. He asked her to start a free school for girls. This fed into her growing vision. Taking a risk, Elizabeth moved with all her children to Baltimore and then to Emmitsburg, Maryland, where in 1809 she opened St. Joseph's Academy for Girls. She knew she'd need teachers. Seeking advice and spiritual guidance from the Catholic communities in Boston, Baltimore, and New York, she formed the first American community of nuns, the American Sisters of Charity. Her school was the seed of what would grow into thousands of parochial schools across America and around the world.

She started with five nuns, but it grew. When she died in 1821, there were fifty sisters in her community. In 1850 they joined with the International Daughters of Charity, bringing the vision of St. Vincent de Paul to America. In 1860, Abraham Lincoln pleaded for and received 200 Daughters of Charity to nurse on Civil War battlefields. Emmitsburg is only seventeen miles from Gettysburg. The kindness and dedication with which the nuns nursed soldiers of both the North and South created a turning point in how the country viewed Catholics.

In 1898, the US government once again put a call out for women to volunteer, this time in the army camps of the Spanish-American War. More than 28,000 soldiers were dead or dying of diarrhea, typhoid fever, and, not least of all, battle wounds. Thousands of women volunteered, but almost none of them were trained. Two hundred and fifty nurses from the Daughters of Charity were among those who took command.

As of 2017, there are 17,000 Daughters of Charity worldwide. Today, HIV/AIDS centers, migrant and refugee assistance, and, especially, schools comprise their mission. How ungrateful I was as a student in the parochial school system! Standing there, I realized that I, too, had personally benefited by this saint's vision: to educate the poor and the middle class.

I darted across the busy street and ducked into Our Lady of the Rosary Church, Mother Elizabeth Ann Seton's shrine. It is very, very plain. White walls, wooden pews, lamps hanging from long chains, small windows, and a small altar, with Mass for about fifty people now well under way. I'd missed the high point of the Mass, the consecration, where the priest actually changes the bread and wine into Jesus's body and blood. People were filing up to receive Communion, a sacrament that is intended to provide a direct infusion of God's grace, making life go a little better, a little easier. Soon it was over. I lingered next to the rough, white-haired priest and overheard him saying to two European tourists. "I get it all the time. They tell me, 'I went to Seton Hall. I went to Seton High in the Philippines. I went to St. Mary's in Illinois.' " The tourists nod knowingly.

I peeked into the shrine's display area, a stark and moldy smelling room in the back offering electrified candles to light and a donation box—front and center—to help with Superstorm Sandy damage. A quaint series of illustrations lined the wall: little magazine prints depicting St. Seton's love for children, her achievements, her trials. And that's about all there was to it, in this minuscule church at the base of these domineering skyscrapers. One day, I'll find myself in Emmitsburg and go see her actual body.

Leaving, I decided to grab a Starbucks and walk back to the hotel, about seventy blocks. Bill would be wondering what was keeping me. I had come to realize that my interest in "seeking" was my thing and, for both of our sakes, I'd stopped wanting him to come along. But when he did ask where I was going, it could be hard to explain because I knew he didn't want the long answer. So usually I'd say, "Oh, you know, just poking around with the saint stuff." Thankfully, he gives me a lot of space.

It was chilly. I had a hot coffee to warm my hands. I passed people who looked homeless hunched on benches, pigeons picking at trash, pretzel vendors setting up shop, geraniums in window boxes, joggers, lovely little gated parks. How could one woman, widowed at twenty-nine with so many children and her fortune lost, create so much? And get the ball rolling for so much more? In Pasadena alone there are four parochial schools and seven more within a stone's throw. We all know women whose lives are all about others—their families, friends, communities—and just think of today's female political, business, educational, and social-justice leaders! But the ladies who achieved the level of saint elevated their practical skills, intellect, drive, and spirituality to a level that far surpassed everyone else around them. Why? How? Does the universe have a deep-space reservoir of energizing spirituality that some people have a special line to? Something that stirs up their hearts and minds and gives them superpowers? Furthermore, why do so many people scoff at a belief in God and spirituality? I'm not thinking about rules and religion, I'm thinking of the opposite: letting oneself go like a helium balloon to be available to intuition, direction, and big love.

Ugh. I gave up trying to figure out how people become saints. It's easier to believe that God actually selected them.

I stopped in front of the Church of St. Peter on Barclay at Church Street, the first Catholic church in New York, where Elizabeth Seton met Bishop John Carroll. The 1785 original church burned down; today, it's a powerful granite Greek revival building from 1835. There's a painting of the crucifixion above the altar, a gift from Mexico in 1789. It is the very one that St. Seton prayed before to draw strength in her times of depression, uncertainty, and anxiety. Two hundred years later, St. Peter's was one of the staging areas for emergency responders after the 9/11 terrorist attacks. The body of Fr. Mychal Judge, chaplain for the New York City Fire Department and officially the first casualty of the attacks, was brought here by fellow firefighters. They laid him right there, before the altar and the painting. When

I read this, my heart ached. St. Seton and 9/11, two such different stories, intersected here. The words above the painting read, "When I am lifted up, I will draw everyone to myself."

I learned something else later that amazed me. While Pope Francis was at the White House, President Obama presented him with a gift: a key. It was St. Elizabeth Ann Seton's house key from her home in Emmitsburg, where she started her school and the Daughters of Charity. President Obama wrote a note to the Pope and attached it to the key saying, "This gift celebrates St. Elizabeth Ann Seton's and your dedication to opening doors for those who are poor, sick, or underserved." Pope Francis took St. Seton's house key home with him.

It was a beautiful walk back up to the hotel. Before I knew it, I was cutting through Central Park and then to 76th and Madison. In a few minutes Bill and I would be having a cappuccino somewhere, talking and thinking about what everybody talks and thinks about: politics, movies, money, what a mess the world is, our kids, our friends.... And somewhere out there I knew, was a woman—no, actually tens of thousands of women—doing what St. Elizabeth Ann Seton did: opening their doors to educate all comers. And they're doing it in every school, in every city, everywhere.

Here is the twelfth-century prayer
so important to St. Seton:

"Memorare"

*Remember, O most gracious Virgin Mary,
that never was it known that anyone who fled
to thy protection, implored thy help, or sought
thy intercession was left unaided. Inspired
with this confidence, I fly unto thee, O Virgin
of virgins, my Mother; to thee do I come; before
thee I stand, sinful and sorrowful.*

*O Mother of the Word Incarnate, despise
not my petitions, but in thy mercy hear and
answer me.*

Amen

Seven

Call Mom!

OUR LADY OF GUADALUPE
1531–present
Mexico City

In the fall of 2016, Rosie, our youngest and a recent college graduate, was trying to figure out her next step. One morning she turned her eyes dolefully toward me. "Mom—would *you* go with me?"

"Me!? But you're leaving the day after tomorrow!"

Bill looked up from across the kitchen, where he was reading the paper. He nodded his head firmly in the affirmative. His silent action spoke loudly: *Go with her. Don't let her go to Mexico City by herself....*

"It's all falling through," Rosie continued. "My friends keep changing their minds, and now they've all backed out." The original plan had been for this group to visit another friend who was on a Fulbright scholarship in Mexico City, but Rosie and her friends had been unable to reach her. Their graduating-from-college celebration trip was falling apart.

"Honey, I...I haven't got an inkling about what Mexico's like anymore—it's been forty years." No pre-trip research...all that drug cartel madness... but Bill had already opened the computer. Checking on Rosie's cheapo flight, which she'd gotten when she and her friends first planned the trip, he found it to be totally full except the seat right next to her. Rapidly I tried to rearrange my mind to get on board with this dramatic twist. If I did go, this harum-scarum trip could offer a chance to see the mystical image of Mary, the Virgin of Guadalupe. Also, how many mothers are lucky enough to have a daughter who *wants* them to join their vacation? "But Rosie," I said, "I'm too old for youth hostels. We need a nice hotel." She nodded. (Hardship? I think not). "And we have to go see the Virgin of Guadalupe." She smiled. Then I smiled.

Who has not seen a picture of *La Virgen*? She's imprinted onto everything from bottlecaps to T-shirts, and her image hangs in every Catholic church in every town in the Americas, from the top of Alaska to the tip of Tierra del Fuego. But the original hangs in a massive basilica in Mexico City. Here's the CliffsNotes on how she came to be in the hearts and minds of millions of people:

An Aztec peasant named Juan Diego walked along Tepeyac Hill on the northern edge of Mexico

City one day in 1531. Before him appeared a vision of a woman wrapped in a blue cloak. She announced herself to be the mother of God. She told Juan Diego to deliver a message to the bishop: She wanted a church to be built on that very spot, and said that if it were built, it would bring about a great Christian conversion. Well, Juan Diego did as he was told, but he trembled all the way to the bishop's palace, afraid that one so lowly as he should ask the great man anything. Spain ruled Mexico then, and the arrogant conquistadors were known for their merciless treatment of the indigenous people. So, naturally, the Spanish bishop scolded and dismissed Juan Diego for wasting his precious time. He was not to return unless he had some proof that Mary had deigned to appear to one so humble.

As he crossed Tepeyac Hill on his way home, Juan Diego was greeted by the shimmering woman again.

"Your Lady, the bishop wants proof," he said sadly.

"Proof? Hmm—okay. My son, see those roses? Gather them into your cloak and carry them back to the bishop." The roses suddenly blooming there were of a type that grew only in Spain. Tepeyac Hill was a dusty, barren place. Juan Diego gathered them into his *tilma*, an Aztec cloak woven of cactus fibers, and returned to the bishop. I can just hear the bishop: "Oh, not *you* again!" Juan Diego opened his cloak and dropped his load of blooming roses before a now-astonished bishop. And Mary had added something more to sweeten the deal: a gorgeous image of herself imprinted onto the inside of his cloak. It is the image we all know today—she stands on a crescent moon, adorned with a blue cape spangled in stars, and she emanates rays of the sun. Her bowed face is brown, that of an Indian. The black band around her waist signifies that she is pregnant, and her unbraided hair signifies that she is unmarried. Mary, the mother of God, is Aztec. Then and there, Spain's superior-imperious worldview was busted. The bishop was so moved by the image that he did as he was told and built a church on Tepeyac Hill. Not only did this conversion of the heart change how the Spanish viewed the Aztecs, but also how the Aztecs behaved. In those days, Aztecs were aggressive warriors, and human sacrifice was rampant. Mary's appearance meant that was no longer going to fly.

Throughout the ages, with her image bubbling up in pancakes and burning through in tortillas (and even scarring the bark of a camphor tree in my own neighborhood), the Catholic church formally acknowledges only three of the thousands upon thousands of Mary sightings and apparitions: Fatima, Lourdes, and Tepeyac Hill.

By jumping in with Rosie on this trip, I'd get to see the famous cloak and further my interest in the lady saints. Because Mary, or Our Lady of Guadalupe as she is known there, is the first and the greatest saint of all. I'd better get packing.

Three and a half hours after leaving LAX, you too could be in an Uber, fearing for your life, as a college-student driver careens through insane traffic. Jumbo billboards shout their messages of—beauty cream! See the big plum shrivel into a pitiful prune—*Don't let this happen to your face!* Or root canals now! Don't wait! Gums cut away, shiny screws, metallic drills, one big word saying it all: *D-E-N-T-I-S-T-A*. Everywhere, everywhere are billboards and beeping, zipping scooters and raucous, zooming cars. It's all a dizzying visual overload. Over here, an office building with stacked floors of giant picture windows showcasing in each a restored vintage Chevy, Oldsmobile, or Impala, like candy in a candy store. Over there, a row of art nouveau buildings leaning into the sides of thrilling new skyscrapers.

Six crisply uniformed doormen greeted us at our hotel and almost fell over themselves trying to outdo one another to help. "Madam, let me get the door."

"No, madam, let me get the door."

"Let me get your bag."

"No, let me get your bag." When I asked where the nearest ATM was, all kinds of arguing broke out over how best to direct me. It was comical, but the shower of attention gave us confidence in Mexico's uncertain landscape.

We felt lucky from the start. First, the November

air was so clear and crisp and clean, in a city that's normally killing itself with pollution. And everyone seemed like extroverts with their energy, their openness, the amount of laughing in restaurants, and their willingness to help a mother-daughter duo from LA. It's fun to bite into something on your breakfast plate and realize you're eating cactus, and to discover that the crunch on top of your dinner is a fried beetle. I began to relax and remember my summer in Mexico in 1974, and the random travel tip that my mother waved me off with as I boarded a Greyhound bus for Guadalajara: "Remember, honey, all Mexicans love children."

We decided to go see *La Virgen* first, before shopping, before pyramids, before museums. The crowds swallowed us up the second we stepped from our Uber, absorbed into the phalanx of the faithful marching up the wide, slick paseo toward the gargantuan basilica that houses Juan Diego's cloak. This church, which some call ugly and others call beautiful, was designed in 1973 by the same architect who did Mexico City's National Museum of Anthropology. It replaced the basilica from the 1700s, which in turn replaced the one from 1550. It accommodates the millions upon millions of people who come to pay homage to *La Virgen* and see the cloak with their own eyes. I was surprised to learn that it's the most visited Catholic site in the world. Ten thousand fit in the church, 50,000 in the courtyard.

People, people, people everywhere, seemingly everyone carrying something big: crosses, tin statues of Guadalupe, banners, giant sodas, ashes of loved ones. It seemed like there were thousands of babies—in arms, in strollers, on the shoulders of their dads—not to mention all the *abuelos* and *abuelas* being pushed in wheelchairs. Poor people sat on the ground by the McDonald's, not far from a shoe store—*zapateria*—that's as ginormous as an IKEA, and just around the corner is a really weird museum of curiosities with a car-size fake (duh) great white shark on the roof along with (why not?) a werewolf in jeans pointing toward the museum's entrance. Rap music blared from snack shops. It suddenly was so, so hot. An altitude headache sprang up. It all became too much. Could this really be the most holy site in the Americas?

We carried on into the grounds of the basilica and crossed a blasting-hot plaza packed with every kind of cheerful youth group, family group, religious group, and pilgrimage group. Was I alone in my turn-off to this chaotic zoo? Was the stinging glare of the sun affecting only me? We waded into the basilica itself, which has been called everything from a flying saucer to a circus tent for its heavy seventies look. Mariachis, loud as you've ever heard them, blasted their happy music from the altar. Mass for 5,000 blared from loudspeakers. I was about to faint. My feet and fingers were swelling up. Water. I needed water. I found a bench to sit on, back in a corner. *Rest*, I told myself. Don't run screaming before witnessing the reason you came. Rosie and I then realized that random priests were stationed all around. You could line up for a blessing. Okay. We waited in line. I calmed down and began to reset myself. I was actually here! No online research, no magazine or pamphlet, could convey the size and overwhelming sensation of this strange vortex of a place. Twenty million people visit each year! I gave myself a pep talk. *Twenty million visitors, that's a good thing. It's a privilege to be among them. Fight for a positive experience. It's up to me what I take away from this day.*

After a priest laid his hands on our heads, we squeezed up to a side altar where there was one of the big, beautiful fake images of Our Lady of Guadalupe. We lit a candle. The real image was still several metal detectors to go. On a high ledge next to the fake image, people had put photos, prayers, and letters of request. It seemed like the right place. I asked Rosie, much taller than me, to reach up to that ledge and put my two-page letter of intentions next to the others.

Early that morning I'd grabbed a coffee in the hotel lobby and settled into a cushy chair to meditate, pray, and prepare myself to view the miraculous image, imprinted by God. My intentions, like those of mothers everywhere, were for the success and protection of my dear children. For my husband and his health and happiness, for all of his family, for all of my siblings and all of their children, and for all of our friends' health and happiness. I petitioned for the fulfillment of the hopes and aspirations of everyone I love or might possibly love. That is what I wanted that day. I'd decided to write it all out in Spanish, so I might have asked for other things, too—Teresa, our Salvadoran housekeeper of more than twenty years, often breaks out laughing after I've "communicated" in Spanish. We both remember the time I asked her for a nose job.

Now into the inner sanctum. We went down a ramp to the lower floor. We went through security and screening. We hopped onto the people mover, like at the airport, and suddenly we were gliding past the 500-year-old cloak, surrounded in gold and hung high above our heads. There she was, snug behind bulletproof glass. The simplicity of the woven garment, and the exact likeness to all the copies, was startling. I stared as hard as I could, wanting to catch all the details: the stars in her cloak that are patterned exactly to the night sky of the date she appeared (December 12, 1531). I studied the black ribbon around her waist. I stared at her parted black hair that flows behind her shoulders. Her dark, love-infused indigenous face that, according to the Bowers Museum in Santa Ana, where I attended a big Guadalupe show, no artist has been capable of capturing. I was gliding past Guadalupe—the actual mystical imprint of the woman who announced herself to be the merciful and understanding mother to us all, the one who said in one of her five apparitions, *"Please, children, come to me with your suffering."*

This sacred image has not faded. It is not dyed. And it has been continuously studied and documented by scientists since it first appeared in Juan Diego's cloak. It's made of cactus fibers, which do not last more than twenty years, yet it hasn't decayed after so many centuries.

All around the world, the Virgin Mary has appeared in dark times: in Fatima, in Rwanda, in sixteenth-century Mexico. Both the Spanish and the Aztec received her message that they were equally her children. She is so beloved by so many for the very directness of her messages. *"For those who love me, I will hear your weeping, your complaints, and heal all your sorrows, hardships, and sufferings. Those who are drawn to me are drawn to my Son."*

As we took our third trip around on the people mover, to saturate ourselves in the site and the experience, I recalled seeing the real Mona Lisa, the real moon rock, and the real crown jewels. This was similar, but booted way up into a palpable sense of communal enthrallment. Rosie and I clasped each other's hands. We stood shoulder to shoulder with those around us. The air seemed alive. I felt like I could hear everyone's mental chattering of fervent prayer, and it was beautiful. Yet my mind fretted back and forth: *It's real. She's real. It can't be. It is. No. Yes. But how? It is. It just is.* This feeling of love, this calm, this pureness—especially among such huge crowds, it doesn't come from nowhere.

When it was time to go, I knew the feeling of utter love and calm we were experiencing would be as difficult to hold as pouring water into a glass full of cracks.

Mexico City is more than 7,000 feet above sea level. The temperature might read a moderate seventy degrees, but the sun is searing, so the shade of our hotel courtyard came as such a relief. Coffee arrived.

I began to think about the Virgin of Guadalupe. No other country has a woman as their spiritual head. And not just one country—in 1996, she was made not just the patron saint of Mexico, or even of all Latin America, but of all the Americas. It was decreed that her image be hung in every Catholic church on both continents. In Mexico, she is *everywhere*: in every home, every Catholic church, on streets, in restaurants. She then began spreading everywhere north and south of Mexico, from walls of liquor stores to murals on freeway underpasses. It's amazing to think that no matter how different people are—a gang member in LA, a housewife in Pasadena, a waiter in Texas, a billionaire in Mexico

City—something they can all agree on is affection for and trust in the Virgin of Guadalupe. That alone feels like a miracle.

The cheapo flight back home was a bit of a payback for all the good luck we'd had. We'd bought so many souvenirs, and darned if we were going to pay to check another bag, so we crammed everything— candles, embroidered dresses, clay horns, bags of hand-decorated matchboxes, mezcal—into our carry-ons, which were so heavy and bulging that we disrupted everyone trying to get to our seats all the way back by the toilets. And, of course, what twenty-two-year-old doesn't come home with a fur coat from a thrift shop? What a scene getting into our tiny seats. But it wasn't nearly the scene that Cathy, a seventy-five-year-old hippie lady, made when she crawled across us in her flouncy dress, floppy hat, and bags hanging off her to get to her window seat. She also carried a furry dog. At least Rosie's fur coat wasn't alive. Cathy, who lived off the grid in a rural town south of Mexico City, was coming up to Glendale to see her grandchildren. She asked if we'd gone to the Museum of Anthropology. I said, Oh, yes, and we'd seen the Virgin of Guadalupe too. She launched in, "Oh, I'm not Catholic, but I love the Virgin. She's become very real to me. I mean, the image is very calming. When I'm seeing the Virgin,

I think, okay, everything is going to be okay. There's a little shrine for her at the end of my dirt road in Amatlan de Quetzalcoatl. I love that she's a woman, not a man." *Me too*, I thought.

Back home, I began to see the Virgin everywhere. When Sylvia, who does my eyelash extensions, noticed the little pin I'd been wearing since I got home, she sighed and whispered, "Oh, Mary Lea, *La Virgen*."

"Yes, Sylvia, yes, I went to see her," I said, bringing back a flood of love inside me.

"Oh my God, would you like to see my tattoo?" she offered. Instantly I thought, *Oh, no, Sylvia has scarred herself.* I hate tattoos.

"Yes, of course, I'd love to see your tattoo," I said. Sylvia pulled up her blouse and pulled down her jeans and, swear ta' God, down her side from her bra line to her panty line was a full-color rendition of the Virgin of Guadalupe—all of it, the stars, the moon, the rays of sun—and it was incredible.

"I gave this to myself for my thirtieth birthday," she said, "when I didn't die."

"Oh my gosh, what happened?"

"I'll tell you about that on your next appointment. You said you wanted to hear how I'm already a grandmother at thirty-six."

A little later I remembered, as if it were brand new, that she was in my garden too. It's a three-foot cement Virgin of Guadalupe that my friend Sherrill told me I needed a few years back when we were shopping at a nursery. The statue in my camellias was not only beautiful, but it started becoming more powerful for me. Because I'd never noticed before how my faithful gardeners, who come each week to mow and blow, always paused to spend a moment with her. To witness their prayer and respect reprimanded me, called me to see the false nature of class separation. She is mother to them, she is mother to me. When I learned that the man who comes to wash our cars was named Jesus, I thought—*What if he really is Jesus?* How would my complete obliviousness to him, except for the service he provides, play out at the pearly gates? Don't we owe more to one another? Witnessing the affection for *La Virgen* from various people brought an opening in my heart that was just not there before. I started making it my business to learn the names of every gardener, every mechanic, every babysitter, every housekeeper I came across. To make sure ice water was on hand, to learn the names of their children and what schools they attended. I became aware of my self-centeredness, and it was embarrassing. These feelings just were not there before my visit to the Virgin.

Saint Everywhere

Recently a young woman named Carol, a friend of Rosie's from high school who's lived with us the past couple of years, reminded me that her middle name is Guadalupe. "Why did your mom give you that name?" I asked.

"Well, I came along unexpectedly, and my mother was worried because she didn't know how she was going to handle a baby. So she prayed to *La Virgen* for it to be all right, for me to be born healthy and happy. And I was! So she named me Guadalupe to give thanks," she said with a chuckle.

Thinking about Guadalupe, who appeared as the mother of us all, the one we can turn to when we're afraid or when things turn awful, makes me realize how few women can actually be that type of mother. I never confided in my mother because she'd just judge and correct me. My grandmother, who lived with us, was so vain that she wouldn't lift a finger around the house, driving my mother nuts. Me, of course, I'm perfect. Well, maybe I care *a little* too much about some things and get *a little* uptight sometimes. My girls call it "going crazy on them." But I've tried to do my best, just as my mother did her best. We all continually try. Falling short and feeling bad is part of our lot. But humanity's been given a gift in the idea of Mary, Our Lady of Guadalupe, who infinitely does not judge, who infinitely says just keep trying, who infinitely advises us to turn to her Son.

Eight

Climbing the Mountain

OUR LADY OF PEACE
1981-present
Medjugorje, Bosnia

It had been fifteen years since I'd seen the visionary from Medjugorje in Glendale. Rosie, who was a fourth grader back then, was out of college now. Bill and I were to meet friends in Venice for the big international contemporary art show, the Biennale. I busily made our plans. Maybe take the roundabout way? Arrive in Paris and take the train to Turin, where the food emporium EATALY is? Oh my gosh, I could see the shroud, too. And the Po River, the river that Bill's father had fought his way up in World War II.

While scanning a map of northern Italy and all the cool places to visit—do we pick Verona or Vicenza or Padova?—my eyes kept wandering farther east to the Adriatic Sea, Zagreb, and Split. Split, where movie stars play. Not far from Split, I spied the little tiny letters M-e-d-j-u-g-o-r-j-e, across the border from Croatia in Bosnia. I'd always thought Bosnia was super far away, but actually, no, not if you're already in Venice. Maybe I could go see for myself. I came up with a plan for an eight-day solo trip, taking a train and an overnight ferry and a bus across Croatia and up into Bosnia. I wanted to see and maybe even experience some of the things I'd heard people talk about. It couldn't be too far off the beaten path if a million people visited every year.

"What? You want to go *where*?" Bill asked, dismayed. "It's so far! It might be dangerous! Why do you even want to?"

"It's...it's an opportunity," was all I could say. He saw I really wanted to go. He sighed. He reluctantly gave me his blessing but with one firm request, "Please plan everything out, so I know exactly where you are, because I won't be there to protect you." Very reasonable. And I loved him for it. After thirty-plus years together, I'd come to realize that his various reluctances were good ballast for me.

That's how I came to be standing alone in the Venice train station as the water taxi pulled away, Bill and I waving to each another as he headed to the airport and home, while I was embarking on a two-day overland trip to Medjugorje. A fifty-minute flight could get you almost there, but that just wasn't enough of a journey for what I had in mind.

The two days would give me a chance to be let loose in the world and experience what it's like to be free, to be a complete stranger. I wondered how much kindness the world might offer up to a sixty-two-year-old woman known by no one.

Well, Bill wasn't gone ten minutes when to my dismay I realized, while standing completely alone in the chaotic train station, that I'd messed up my internet train ticket: It was for tomorrow, not for right now—my train with a switch in Bologna, my train to a nonrefundable hotel for that night, to an already-paid space on the ferry, to a reserved bus ticket from Split to Medjugorje, to a pre-paid hotel there. *I had to be on that train in half an hour, not tomorrow!*

The Italian rail system couldn't give a rat's ass about one little person's problem. I tried to wait politely to get to the reservations window. Finally, I was face to face with the clerk, asking for a ticket change, pleading to be understood—but he looked straight through me. I was nothing to him. He chatted with a coworker, sipped something, and turned to flip through a stack of papers. Clock ticking! Wow, he was shining me on! He looked at the clock and put up a little "closed" sign right in my face. The horrible words *Fuck you!* roared up in my mind as he strolled away.

I raced to the automated kiosk. Making a quick decision, I forwent a ticket change or a rebate and decided to take the loss and just get a ticket for now. Five minutes to go. I fed all of my cash into the kiosk (credit card slot, broken), which spit out only one leg of the train trip. Crap! Okay, figure that out in Bologna! I ran, I sweated, I harrumphed my giant suitcase up the ladder and jumped onto the Venice-Bologna train just as it started to roll. I stumbled in the aisle and bruised my leg. My white shirt had smudges down the front from my suitcase. I was so sweaty and stinky I wanted to cry.

I didn't want to sit next to a man for the three-hour ride. Finally I found two young women who were facing each another in a four-seat configuration. They yakked away, back and forth, intermittently pausing for furious texting and searching on their phones. College girls? They were oblivious toward me or anyone else: just texting, texting, looking at each other, talking, and then, heads down and texting again.

I coughed out, *"Permisso? Signorinas?* English?" They paused, slightly frowning, glanced at each another, and shook their heads, "No." But then, reluctantly, one said, "What is it?"

I cleared my throat again, nervous. "Could you tell me where the train station is in Ancona? I'm going to"—I pulled out my Expedia confirmation—"this hotel." I wanted to confirm that it was as close to the train station as I'd been told. She took the paper from me. "I Google it," she said. Okay, we'd all lived in the digital age a good fifteen years by then, but I was still amazed at how swiftly she had it. "Lady, here." She showed me. The blue line on the Google Maps screen crawled its way a long, long way across the city of Ancona from the train station to the hotel. Crap. She saw my face. "Maybe call hotel," she said. I took out my phone: Oh God, technology—how to make a local but international call? What plan did I have again? Bill takes care of so much for me. I tried to look efficient. I tried to make the call. I tried again. Anxiety was rearing its head. So far this whole trip was nothing but NOT FUN. Bill must be up in the air, relaxing in his business-class seat. I waved the phone weakly.

"I call," she said, taking my confirmation. In no time she had the hotel on the phone, and when she finished, she said, "Lady. Okay. Google make a mistake. One mile from train station is all. They await you."

Then a young man across the aisle said, "Si, si, Google many times is not right. Where you from, lady?"

"California," I replied. "In California, Google is always right." That made all three of them laugh.

"In Italy, not. Ah, and why you alone, lady?" the helpful girl now wanted to know. "Very far from California." I didn't want to say I was three hours into an eight-day personal retreat. I didn't want to tell them I'd asked God to be my traveling companion.

"Oh, I'll be meeting friends," I said vaguely, so they wouldn't worry for me.

The boy across the aisle said, "California. I l-o-v-e California so much. I will go there after I graduate. That's why I study energy, so I can one day live in California." He said this with such hope for a golden place, where everything works out like in a dream.

A glance out the window: beautiful Italy passing by. I'd made the train. The hotel was real and they were awaiting me. The attitude took hold that getting the next ticket from Bologna on through to Ancona would work out. These college kids couldn't have known how anxious I'd been, what their small actions had done to help me. I apologized, in my head, for having cursed at the reservation clerk.

We pulled into Bologna. Suddenly everyone bolted out of their seats to push their way off the train. The kids were gone, and I was being run over by people racing past me. My big fat suitcase got swept out of my hands. *Get it! Get the suitcase before it's gone!* I went white-hot with fear. It was gone!

A bulky man hopped off the train and put himself right in front of the steep steps. *He's the one who snatched my suitcase.* Breaking into a sweat, I called, "No, no, no!" He quickly stepped aside from the suitcase and made that very Italian gesture of throwing his hands open and then down as if to say, *Here ya go—it's all yours.* He nodded a good day, picked up his own bags, and was gone. Clumsily, I got ahold of my bag and smiled a thanks to the back of his head. I took a deep breath. Wow, he'd had his own luggage to deal with, and the station was so crowded and pushy.... It was so nice of him to lift my bag down the steps!

But Bologna's train station was worse than Venice's! I quickly encountered freaky-long underground corridors of rushing people, hustlers begging money, unhelpful clerks, and confusing signage. But how helpful that man was to have gotten my suitcase off for me. Soon I was on the next train from Bologna to Ancona (credit cards worked here). I'd be there by dark. I settled down and began thinking about Mary.

My deeper interest in her started just before the birth of our third child. I was almost forty-two. We had two healthy children. Was it greedy of me to want another? Would this be the time bad things happened? I heard of a lady who had a stroke right on the delivery table! And another who had one blue eye and one brown eye, and her baby was born with just one eye! What about a cord around the neck? Oh, it was endless. This was before I'd encountered the baby Jesus of Prague, so I was regularly tormenting myself with anxious thoughts. But three weeks before delivery, a phrase popped into my mind: "If Mary can do it in a barn, I can do it at the Huntington" (our nice hospital in Pasadena). It went through my head over and over and over. "If Mary can do it in a barn, I can do it at the Huntington." Well, it all went perfectly: a ten-pound baby, labor an hour and forty-five minutes. I really felt divine assistance in bringing this baby into the world, and I began turning to the idea of Mary with motherhood problems. It helped a lot. What mother doesn't need more confidence, calm, and perseverance?

Also, not long after this time, Mary helped me win a diamond in a raffle. We used to get *The Tidings*, the free Catholic newspaper for the Los Angeles area. I'd peruse it from time to time, and one day there was an ad from a church in the Midwest announcing: "Win a $10,000 diamond! Only 250 tickets will be sold!" I bought a ticket because a picture of the Virgin Mary was part of the ad. I looked hard at the ad, weirdly knowing I was going to win. Without telling Bill, I wrote a check for $200 and sent it off. We definitely did not have that kind of money back then, and I only told him about it when I actually had the sparkling one-carat diamond in the palm of my hand. Of course, that's no sign of anything but luck, but it still made me like Mary even more.

She is a saint despite it all: having to pick up everything and flee, having a son who was *different*, having a son who was murdered. She is the saint who understands human troubles, all aspects of home and family life. She surmounted her personal grief to be a woman for others. She also figured out how to enjoy life, to keep the fun going by asking her

Son to do *something* about there being no more wine.

Apparitions of Mary happen all over the world, across cultures and religions. There are more mentions of Mary, or Maryam, in the Qur'an than in the New Testament, where she actually speaks only four times, yet today, she is the confidante of billions of people and is known by so many names: Our Lady of Guadalupe, Our Lady of Fatima, Our Lady of Grace, Our Lady of Solitude, Mystical Rose, and Mother of Mercy, as well as the Untier of Knots, the Refuge of Sinners, and so on. I was on my way to visit Our Lady of Peace, as she is called in Medjugorje. In all of her appearances, Mary, the Mother of All Saints, has basically asked two things: that we each bring more love to one another, and that we pray the rosary. So I sat there staring out the window, and as we skirted the beach towns of the Italian Adriatic, I said the rosary.

Thank you, God. Thank you, God. I arrived at the Sea Port Hotel, from which you can see the port of Ancona. The hotel was so clean, so modern, so welcoming. I knew it wasn't personal, but I felt like it had been waiting all day *just for me*! I felt the deep reason for hotels: to provide shelter, safety, and hospitality. When traveling alone, it's tremendously helpful to have a welcoming place to stay. I'd made it. On paper, my day looked like no big deal: take the train from Venice to Ancona and check into a hotel just a short cab ride from the train station. But it was a big deal. I had stepped off the edge of my regular life, solo, and was wending my way farther and farther away from all that I knew. And I didn't have much of a plan.

I took a shower. Put on clean clothes. Strolled up to the rooftop lounge. Oh, the sun setting over the Adriatic! It was exciting to say the word *Adriatic*. I could see a cathedral on the hill, and giant ferries were lined up in the harbor below, stoking up for their nightly runs to Athens, Dubrovnik, and Split (me, tomorrow night). I found a stool at the railing. Really, the pink streaking sunset, the lights twinkling in the hills, and the balmy summer air were all too beautiful for one person alone. It plunged me into loneliness for Bill, or for any other person even, to just exclaim about the beauty. I went into my mind and asked God to please be good enough company on this trip. Keep me from being lonely.

And then, "Madam, cocktail?" asked the waitress, a sparkling young Russian woman with spiky hair.

"Yes!" I replied, like I'd just won on a game show. "It's so beautiful here, isn't it?"

"Okay!" she answered. Her sparkle broke into laughter as I waved my arms and cupped my hands, trying to capture the view and hold onto it.

"White wine, please!" And we both continued to laugh because of the gorgeous view. She waved her arms too, just for fun.

"I so glad to live Italy," she said. "My son. My family. Now all here Italy. It my dream." Irena was her name, I found out. I'd learned my lesson on the train. I hadn't gotten the names of any of the college kids or the man who helped and now, how can I properly appreciate them?

"Thank you, Irena," I said when she came back with a big, frosty glass of wine. She laughed again. I laughed. Maybe that's the language we will speak. She returned again soon, this time bringing some pizza and polenta on small plates. "A surprise you." She laughed. I laughed. The sun was going down, and so was Day One.

It's terrible to have too much luggage. My suitcase was the biggest available at T.J. Maxx because, well, I thought I needed it all. Woefully, I stared at the three stories of steps up, up, up to the thousand-person ferry before me. I looked around. I mustered myself. "Oh, young man? Excuse me, young man?" Three young men, traveling with backpacks, all turned around. They were also waiting to board. "Can I buy you some beers this evening to hoist this suitcase up the flights of steps, please?" They all spoke German, and they all offered to help...and I'd find them somehow later. I was to share a cabin with three other ladies, as every single cabin was already booked. Whatever, it was only for one night. But as I eyed everybody as they checked in, it dawned on me that this overnight ferry to the Croatian islands was one gigantic party bus. There were several bars, a casino, and, of course, the party deck for those who weren't buying berths but would sit up all night drinking, like the young Germans.

The woman at check-in looked me over frankly. "Madam," she said, "you may be more comfortable in a single, on a higher floor—and I have a cancellation."

"Well, that's incredible. Thank you! How much more is it?" I asked.

Shaking her head, she said, "Nothing. Have a good trip to Medjugorje."

"How did you know that's where I'm going?" I asked, surprised. She smiled.

"You look the type."

After dumping my stuff and taking a shower in what really seemed like a sink, that without care would have soaked my entire little berth, I put on fresh clothes and went to find the Germans to make good on my offer. The open-air party deck was in full swing, with cabana bars set up on the edges, kids rolling out sleeping bags, and lovers kissing at the railing. We were already sailing away from Ancona, and the magenta sunset was beginning to glow with stars. It was an almost-hot summer night, and wonderful dance music from the loudspeakers thrilled me with the thought, *Oh, to be young again*. I found the German boys, already well into a few beers, and, feeling brave and adventurous for just being there, approached them and bought them a round. I retreated very soon. I wanted to tuck myself into my cozy berth, listen to the sounds of the ship, say my prayers, and wonder what Split, with its Roman ruins, would be like. (Beautiful.)

The bus from Split, up the cliffs that separate the Croatian coast from the country's central plateau, was so white-knuckle that I changed seats, hoping my weight would keep us from plunging over the edge. The skinny road switch-backed up and up, with no railing between us, the cliffs, and the ocean below. But once we were up and into the valley, a lovely, unusual peace descended upon me. We were on a lovely, unspoiled open road ringed with distant blue mountains, with views of small, haphazard farms, orchards, and flocks of goats and sheep. I had no idea where I was, or what direction we were going. Just that I was on the bus that said "Medjugorje." Or so I thought.

Up until 1981, Medjugorje was nothing more than a village of 400 poor farmers. Back in 1967, they'd worked very hard to build a proper church for themselves, as all they'd had before was a tiny chapel. People laughed because the church, St. James, was so preposterously big (but just average for the United States). Medjugorje's people couldn't say why they wanted such a large church, they just did. Today, because of the apparitions, St. James has an addition with seating for an additional 5,000, as well as a plaza, complete with loudspeakers, that can hold about 2,000 more.

It started with two kids who went up the hill outside of town one summer day in 1981 (to smoke, they admitted later). From a distance, they saw a beautiful woman, bathed in light, hovering just above the ground. They got scared and ran away. The next day, they brought four friends to see if she would appear again. So it was six kids, mostly teenagers, who saw, and mostly still see, the apparitions of Our Lady. She has given them messages for nearly four decades. Officially, the Church doesn't acknowledge what occurs there. It's still in a wait-and-see period.

How casually my old friend Teresa had offered that invitation to go see Ivan Dragicevic so long ago in Glendale, I mused, *and look where it has taken me.* The ride through that valley had such a tranquil-izing effect. Sure, I was preconditioned by desire, but, regardless, I could feel a giant, soft cloak spread high above the vast valley, like the whole place was holy. It was nine p.m. when the bus pulled into the station. I hefted my suitcase from the luggage bay, stood there in the street, and took a deep breath to collect myself. Bill and my safe life were so far away. A nice woman in a convenience store directed me to my hotel, and before long I had settled into my room. It was time to shower. I'd figure it all out tomorrow. I wished I'd done more research on what to do here besides pray. I'd heard stories about how the sun spins and the smell of roses hits you if you're lucky. How the clouds can form strange shapes. How arthritis and cancer can disappear from someone's body. But this didn't help me know what to actually *do* here. My last thought before falling asleep was that I was glad breakfast was included.

But at breakfast, I sat in the completely empty dining room, drinking good-enough coffee and eating scrambled eggs, wondering...how would this all work out? I didn't know a soul. Should I start by taking a walk? Or talking to the lady at the desk? Or—just then, a woman with red hair and a suitcase entered, got her breakfast, and sat down to read.

"Excuse me, ahem—excuse me?" I called politely. She smiled and looked up. "I just arrived last night. Do you have any tips?" She cracked a huge smile.

"This is my fourth time here," she said with a thick Irish accent. "I'm leaving in an hour. If you're brand new here, you must call this woman and tell her you're a friend of Kathleen's. She'll take care of you." She dug in her purse to hand me the business card of someone named Zeljka Rozic. "Pay her as well as you can—people struggle here." I'd call her right after breakfast. I learned that Kathleen's first trip, ten years ago, had been with a group of mothers who came to pray for their families. Kathleen had been coming back on her own ever since.

Before long, Zeljka Rozic (just say "Zilcha") arrived in her old Mercedes-Benz. Her English was perfect, and with her blond hair, she could have been an Orange County mom. She'd once worked in international business, she said, but her children needed her to be home more. She'd fallen into tour guiding because one of her cousins was a visionary. "Welcome," she said so cheerfully. "It's so nice to meet you." In one instant, I knew my time here was going to be fine. The lady saints always said, "With God, everything will be fine." But I say, "With other people, everything will be fine."

"Here, take a bulletin. A new one comes out every day. And if you want an extra headset, take this. No need to pay extra. Give it back when you leave." She handed me headphones and a transistor, which I stowed in my backpack. The bulletin gave a rundown of what spiritual events were happening in Medjugorje.

"Let's take a little drive," she said. I hopped in without concern, and we began chatting like old friends. "Maybe you should start with the church," she said. "How about I drop you off, and I'll be back in two hours. Then there's time to climb Apparition Hill. Would you like that?"

"Yes! I'll see or do whatever you think," I said, putting myself totally in her hands.

Medjugorje is big enough for a few streetlights, a couple of big hotels, some cafés and restaurants, and more Mary on sale than you can imagine. Driving up to St. James, we passed tiny shop after tiny shop, each selling Mary statues, prayer books, racks and racks of rosaries, and kneelers. And you know what? It wasn't trashy; it was all clean and respectful, and the music coming into the streets from all these shops was uplifting classical music, not loud, not beat-driven. It gave a floating, peaceful, Shangri-la feeling to everything. Was this a tourist trap? I'd never been in a place where commerce and tourism were so completely given over to spiritual fulfillment. I mean, we passed Grace Hotel and Hotel Peace. Filling the sidewalks were large groups: here came one wearing purple T-shirts saying "Brazil" and another in yellow T-shirts saying "Korea" and another saying "Italy." A group, led by a priest, of maybe fifty teenage boys and girls, dressed like typical teenagers anywhere, passed by. Everyone was coming toward or away from St. James Church, smack in the center of town. Zeljka let me off in front of the enormous plaza, the center for all the Masses, choir groups, international guest speakers, parades, healing services, and open-air confessions. If I put on the headphones and turned the transistor to channel five, no matter what language was being preached, I could hear it in English. Nifty. And it worked all over town. So *that's* why so many people were wearing headphones, even while having coffee in cafés.

A weird sensation came over me after she dropped

me off in the plaza. I could not make myself move. My feet were stuck to the pavement. It was all very real and unreal. It almost felt like a sci-fi movie. Everyone around me was praying, sitting on benches, walls, or steps, their heads bowed or staring off, or their arms around someone else. I felt like I could read minds, hear all the prayers. I saw that even those whose minds were occupied elsewhere were being bathed in the prayers of others.

I took a seat in front of the Mary statue on the plaza. I don't know why, but I could hardly catch a breath. I just sat there, breathed, and watched other people praying. It wasn't just women praying—there were plenty of men, young and old. It was fascinating to see so many men praying, because at home it's mostly women who pray, in public at least. A little girl walked into my view wearing a prim floral dress and lacy socks, her hair in a tight ponytail. She carried a sparkly purse. Maybe she was six. She walked up to the statue of Mary, knelt down, and blessed herself. She wasn't being told to do this—I spied her mother in the shade, fanning herself and talking to a friend. The purity of this little child was so powerful. I wanted to be as pure and as innocent as she was. Full of grace is what she looked like, untouched by disappointment, by cynicism. I loved watching her, with her little bowed head and clasped hands. Then she got up and ran around.

Glancing at the daily bulletin, I saw there'd

be various Masses and vigils and meditations and speakers all day, but somehow just being here was plenty. I didn't need to run around attending things. I just wanted to be here and inhale this entrancing air. When Zeljka came back for me, she said with a laugh, "You didn't get very far."

It was incredible to have someone appear and just take you where you need to go. Within twenty minutes we were in the suburbs where the hill is, the hill on which the apparitions began. Again, Zeljka let me out of her car.

"Mary Lea, when you come back from the top of the mountain, just catch one of the taxis over there back to your hotel. It'll cost about $5. How about I see you tomorrow morning?" We nodded in happy agreement. I noticed a little outdoor café with cheerful oilcloth draped on its tiny tables. I knew I'd be having a cappuccino there later. I turned from the road to navigate a few rough little streets before getting to the base of Apparition Hill.

There was one last rosary stall before the base of the uphill trail. A group of handsome young men in utility vests waited. When people arrived in wheelchairs or with oxygen tanks, they'd just pick them up, fireman style, and carry them up the trail. Other pilgrims took off their shoes and socks to experience the sharp rocks. One man carried his very old father on his back. I kept my head down, navigating the rocky path, those scenes too intense for me to want to watch. Apparition Hill is just sharp, brown, jutting rocks. The path is mostly an every-man-for-himself scramble up the side of the hill, but lovely Stations of the Cross are built in here and there. I still don't know how long the hike was, maybe an hour, I can't really say, but it felt hard to me, although young people seemed to leap from rock to rock. Like everything in life, of course, you finally get there.

I rounded a curve and it brought me out on top. The simplicity of the scene stopped me in my tracks. Maybe a hundred people sitting, kneeling, or standing around a basically life-size statue of Mary on a pedestal. Just rocks, and air, and prayer, and Mary. It was completely silent. I felt like I had to tiptoe. I found a crazy-hard rock to sit on, kind of near a shrub that cast a tiny bit of shade. I bowed my head. I couldn't really think or say prayers. I just absorbed and let myself be fully in this place at this moment, nowhere else. I tried to breathe deeply, but again, it was difficult, as if what I breathed in was too intense. After a while, I wanted to come closer to the statue, so I navigated my way to my knees on the sharp rocks. I clasped the little metal railing that surrounds the statue. It was definitely not the statue, not even Mary, that I felt wash over me—it was God. I felt profoundly physically weak, like I could barely grasp the railing. Even though I had trouble breathing, I experienced a great feeling within me that shut out the rest of the world, like I was in a tiny closet filled with a powerful, grounding, wonderful sensation. The very deepest part of me—the deepest part of my soul—was being acknowledged, dimming and trivializing everything of this world.

Certainly this was why so many people came here. Why I was 6,402 miles from home. Strange to go all this way for a *feeling*. But honestly, the depth and beauty of what I felt were beyond all previous experience. If I could have hugged the ground, I would have. If I could have stayed in that moment forever, I would have. But when the time came to head down, I did so, if slowly. I said my prayers: gratitude prayers, love prayers, request prayers, thank-you prayers.

After a cappuccino at the tiny corner table at the bottom of the hill, where I could see far across the valley with its wonderfully crooked orchards and fields of gold and buff green and, beyond that, the blue, blue points of the far-off mountains—after that cappuccino, I hailed a taxi. Theodore, the driver, turned to me as we took off and asked in his gruff voice, "Where you from?"

"California."

"Ouff!" he said flourishing his hands. "So far! You came for the Virgin?"

"Yes. Yes I did."

"Good. Very good. Thank God for the Virgin. She brings a lot of money to us. Or else we are poor as the rest of Bosnia. Very good." Theodore drove his old Mercedes cab right through all the potholes and bumps in the road with gusto.

Over the next few days I did attend all the events, and Zeljka kept taking me around. I learned that those young men who help the elderly and ill up the hill are all recovering addicts from Cenocolo, the rehab center in town that attracts addicted men from around the world, making their lives good again. The rehab's magic mix is prayer, hard work, and friendship. Cenocolo was started by one little Italian nun in the 1990s, and now there are centers in Florida, Brazil, and the Philippines.

Zeljka and I had coffee a couple of times. (Travel tip: When traveling alone, always be ready to buy someone coffee.) She explained the ins and outs of the Balkan war of the 1990s. The years when I'd been happily at home raising my children. She cautioned me that the rosy-tinted glasses through which I viewed everything in Medjugorje did not reflect the pickpocket problem, the real poverty outside of the faith tourism, and the way Muslims and Catholics are trying their best to get along with one another. "For now, things are going okay. Everyone seems to want peace," she said. "But it is very hard for the average person. So many cannot even afford an air conditioning unit. This causes stress." I listened to her, awash in gratitude for the life I have.

But Mary appeared here, in this recently strife-torn valley, to once again bring God's message to all of us. One of her thousands of messages is:

*Today I will speak to you about what you
have forgotten. That I am with you. That the
Great Love sends me.*

*I am asking you to recognize love in your
brother. Only in this way, through love, will
you see the face of the Great Love.*

To me, Great Love is a very workable definition
of God. No matter where you're coming from in your
beliefs, doesn't everybody want love?

On my last night in Medjugorje, before head-
ing to Dubrovnik by bus the next morning, I sat on
the Grace Hotel patio, having dinner with Cindy, a
friend I'd made. She'd come here on her own, never
having traveled much and leaving her husband and
children back in Texas. She'd come to pray for her
twenty-two-year-old son, who'd developed schizo-
phrenia, exacerbated, she believed, by all the pot
he'd smoked before he dropped out of college. We
ate dinner, sipped wine, and talked. We prayed
together for strength and wisdom. She wanted to
bring this problem, mother to mother, to Mary's
feet. It was just sunset, and we were going to a vigil
later. I looked up into the telephone wires above us.
Lined up on the wires was a flock of doves. Doves,
not pigeons, were the street bird here.

"Have you been to the weeping Jesus?" Cindy
asked. I said no, I actually hadn't heard of it. She
said, "Oh my gosh, you can't leave without seeing it.
Let's go now." So we paid our bill and walked about

a quarter of a mile back into an open-space garden, where we encountered a gathering of people.

The weeping Jesus (officially the *Risen Christ of Medjugorje*) is a ten-foot bronze statue of the crucifixion made by Andrei Ajdic in 1998 and installed here in 2000. A few years later, people started seeing liquid drip from Jesus's knee, and no one knows how. Scientists say it is not water but is more closely related to the chemical makeup of tears. We got in line to await our turn to draw close to the statue. When it was my turn to approach, I did so cautiously, knowing I was entering into something so strange. I dabbed the liquid on my head and my body. I began to pray, and the world fell away—the other people, time, even contact with myself—evaporated as a powerful, deep, dense feeling of...what? The only way I can describe it is love between me and God. Just me and just God, locked in a ring I never wanted to leave, a ring that came down and around me. Words faded as pure, undiluted feelings communicating nothing but the profoundest knowing, the profoundest sense of being alive, filled everything in me. I was not *in* love, I *was* love. How long did I stand there? A minute, an hour, a year? Eventually someone tapped me on the shoulder. The line had gotten really long. Everyone wanted a turn at bliss, and I stepped away. Could this be what the saints felt? Had I touched, for a moment, the saints' experience? How each had said in her own way that

SAINT EVERYWHERE

she was totally filled with God's love?

It was my last night in Medjugorje. How could I leave? I wasn't done yet. I went back to my hotel and made hasty arrangements to stay one day longer, to take one last bit of time to be someplace so different from where I live. The gentleness of everyone I encountered in those four days in Medjugorje—the hotel staff, shopkeepers, taxi drivers, fellow pilgrims—was so palpable that I actually wondered if heaven was like this.

The thought of going home was a little scary. How could I possibly live at this sublime frequency? And, too, I felt my long journey of discovery was drawing to a close. How could I explain where my mind had been? How could I share with my friends and family all the tiny, powerful experiences that the lady saints I'd visited had given me? I hadn't talked about my experiences with anyone. It had been my fun, inner trip that had shown me how much there is to being alive. Every day gives us the chance to walk out onto the water of a new experience. Every day is an opportunity to feel a powerful love of God.

Maybe, just maybe, I could do something I'd always wanted to do, write a book. I thought of my writing desk back home. I thought of my rose garden. I thought of the lovely, curmudgeonly man I've been married to for thirty-two years. And I thought, *Yeah, thank you, lady saints, for showing me just how much is out there.*

Epilogue

I've been asked if I've felt changed by spending this amount of time and effort on the lady saints. And the answer is, of course! A quiet question keeps coming to me. Could *I* actually do more? What if I have much more capacity than I know? Having spent so much time with these astonishing women makes me want to improve myself. Better, more generous thoughts. Better words spoken. Better action.

My fear, though, is that while this book is slim, the path the lady saints have put me on is long. They don't want to be confined to so few pages, and thus, they keep popping up everywhere. For instance, when I recently tagged along with Glennie on her business trip to New York City, I met Jean. From

Senegal. An Uber driver. He picked me up in his immaculate car, with the coolest jazz playing. Once he started driving, I noticed a plastic rosary wound around his hand, which he kept on the steering wheel. After I got the PhD lecture on the origins of jazz and how his Wall Street successes had imploded after 2008, I commented on the rosary. He gave a deep, rich, French-accented chuckle and said, "Oh, whenever I get a ride that takes me all the way to the top of Manhattan, I stop at the Cabrini Shrine."

"You do?!" I exclaimed.

"I'm an immigrant. She was an immigrant. I talk to her, you know? It helps. Life is really, really hard here in the States." Before I began my travels with the lady saints, this exchange would have been almost meaningless to me, but ever since then, I've been thinking about Jean and his life and his talks with the saint, and hoping he is okay.

Or when I asked Carol, Rosie's friend who lived with us while preparing for medical school, how she got a full scholarship to Mayfield, the private high school where she and Rosie became friends, she said, "The sisters at my grade school came to me in the eighth grade and said they would pay all the tuition for any private high school I could get into, as long as it was Catholic."

"You're kidding. Any school?" I asked. She nodded.

"Carol, but *who were those nuns?*"

"Daughters of Charity," she replied simply.

Daughters of Charity—Elizabeth Ann Seton's order! It absolutely amazed me that 200 years after her death, Elizabeth Ann Seton had profoundly affected the life of this precious young woman who was sitting at my own kitchen table.

Friends have been asking which saint I want to find next. There are so many. Really. It turns out that amazing women lifting up our world are everywhere, all around us, right now. There's the friend who took it upon herself to turn a trashy, ravaged vacant lot into a garden. Or the woman who quit her lucrative real estate career to build an after-school program for kids who had nowhere to go. Or the woman who cooks for twenty-five every Wednesday night and hauls her pots to the park for those who gather there.

These acts may seem pale compared to the billions upon billions donated by Melinda Gates, Priscilla Chan, and Susan Buffett. The words from Priscilla about why she and husband Mark Zuckerberg are giving away 99% of their Facebook stock were simple but mind-bogglingly awesome: "To make the world a better place." And with these gals, I do believe they mean the *whole world*. But tiny, tiny personal acts are also impressive in their own way.

One woman I know decided—don't laugh—to simply smile at everyone she passed. Not because she was so happy but because she wanted to create a more welcoming world. This small action backs up a quote from St. Mother Teresa of Calcutta: "A smile is an act of love."

Another woman I know decided it was time to become a better friend to those already in her life. Not because she was bubbling with energy to see everyone but because she realized that in the end, all we have is one another, and honoring and nurturing that is a way to bring more connection and value to life.

I know a woman who decided to mentally bless every homeless person she passed and envision them in healthy bodies and minds.

Another acquaintance decided to talk to at least one stranger every day, not because she liked all those people in the elevator but because she thought it might help bring a little more trust into our society.

So now I am looking to encounter St. Everywhere. And this, of course, requires no travels...but Bill *did* just say, "Mary Lea, isn't it time we take a little trip?"

Acknowledgments

Things of a creative nature can so easily not happen. When you are literally pulling ideas out of the air, the encouragement and enthusiasm of others becomes essential. Janet Nippell, my brilliant mom-friend and poet, edited each story and thoughtfully talked me through the structure and numerous rewrites. Mel Malmberg invited me into her writers' group at just the right time to boost this project. Her intellect is so acute that when she offered to be a first reader, my instant thought was, *May as well put my feet to the fire right off the bat.*

With a thumbs-up from Mel, I felt ready to look for a publisher. Colleen Dunn Bates runs a beautiful publishing house right here in Pasadena. The themes of this book are not her norm, but she went out on a limb with me, simply stating, "This book deserves to be published." Her dedicated staff—Dorie Bailey, Caitlin Ek, Katelyn Keating, and freelance editor Margery Schwartz—worked with great professionalism to make Colleen's vision a reality.

Thank you, Joe Rohde, for saying yes without hesitation to creating the whimsical illustrations. And thanks to cover designer David Ter-Avanesyan and book designer Amy Inouye for crafting something beautiful.

I also want to acknowledge my Prayer Sisters. We are a group of about ten women who've been meeting for twenty-plus years to keep our prayer life going. Our children were in diapers when we began. Our discussions and moments of inspiration have been so important to me.

So from the bottom of my heart, I thank all these talented individuals, each of whom helped me turn twenty years of scraps and notes and journal entries into a book.

Last but not least, let me wrap my arms around my husband, Bill, and our lovely daughters, Glenn Mary, Grace, and Rosie. I've done my best to form them into sturdy travelers all, so that as my years advance, I'll never be without curious, fun travel companions. Thank you, family, for giving me so much material for these pages and (far more importantly) for being the people God had in store for me.

About the Author

MARY LEA CARROLL worked in travel, the theater, and Hollywood before raising her children. During that time, she also taught children's creative writing and helped with her husband's movie-advertising business. A storyteller and a contributor to the book *Hometown Pasadena*, Carroll is a lifelong resident of Pasadena, California, and a graduate of San Francisco State University.

About the Illustrator

JOE ROHDE is executive designer and vice president of Walt Disney Imagineering.

CPSIA information can be obtained
at www.ICGtesting.com
Printed in the USA
LVHW111640270922
729404LV00003B/153